Living in Hope

KENNON L. CALLAHAN, PH.D.

Copyright © 2015 *Living in Hope* by Dr. Kennon L. Callahan, Ph.D.
All rights reserved. Published in the United States of America.

No part of this book may be used or reproduced in any manner whatsoever without written permission of the author, except in the case of brief quotations embodied in critical articles and reviews.

For information, contact Dr. Kennon L. Callahan, Ph.D.
The National Institute for Church Planning and Consultation,
PMB 280, 381 Casa Linda Plaza, Dallas, Texas 75218

Library of Congress Cataloging in Publication Data
Library of Congress Control Number: 2015914023
CreateSpace Independent Publishing Platform
North Charleston, South Carolina

Callahan, Ph.D., Dr. Kennon L.
Living in Hope.

1. Life.   2. Missions.   3. Leadership.   4. Hope   I. Title
     2015
ISBN-10: 1516998847
ISBN-13: 9781516998845

15   16   17   18   19   20   22   24

Living in Hope

Wherever we find hope,
We find grace and peace.

These three are good friends.

These three gifts bless our lives.

DR. KENNON L. CALLAHAN, B. A., M. DIV., S.T.M, PH.D.

THE TRILOGY

LIVING IN GRACE

LIVING IN PEACE

LIVING IN HOPE

Table of Contents

Dedication of *Living in Hope* ix

Scriptures on Hope xi

Words of Appreciation xv

   1. Julie 1

   2. Mrs. Lott 11

   3. You 17

   4. Strengths 25

   5. Motivations 35

   6. Generosity 49

   7. Passion 53

   8. Memories 61

   9. Mentors 69

  10. Some Changes 77

  11. Outcomes 85

  12. War and Hope 93

  13. Hope 105

  14. Cast Your Nets 115

15. Gossip, Apathy, Generations 121

16. Always 133

17. Encouraging.. 141

18. God's Generous Gift.. 153

About the Author.. 163

1954 Picture of Dr. and Mrs. Callahan 166

Current Picture of Dr. and Mrs. Callahan 167

Bibliography of the Books by the Author................................. 169

This work

is

dedicated to

JULIE MCCOY CALLAHAN

love of my life, good friend, wonderful wife

her grace and compassion,
peace and calm,
hope and encouragement,
wisdom and common sense,
bless my life and the lives of many

Scriptures on Hope

Romans 12:12
Rejoicing in hope; patient in tribulation; continuing instant in prayer.

Jeremiah 29:11
For I know the thoughts that I think toward you, saith the LORD, thoughts of peace, and not of evil, to give you an expected end.

Romans 15:13
Now the God of hope fill you with all joy and peace in believing, that ye may abound in hope, through the power of the Holy Ghost.

Deuteronomy 31:6
Be strong and of a good courage, fear not, nor be afraid of them: for the LORD thy God, he [it is] that doth go with thee; he will not fail thee, nor forsake thee.

Romans 5:2-5
By whom also we have access by faith into this grace wherein we stand, and rejoice in hope of the glory of God. *(Read More...)*

Isaiah 40:31
But they that wait upon the LORD shall renew [their] strength; they shall mount up with wings as eagles; they

shall run, and not be weary; [and] they shall walk, and not faint.

Isaiah 41:10

Fear thou not; for I [am] with thee: be not dismayed; for I [am] thy God: I will strengthen thee; yea, I will help thee; yea, I will uphold thee with the right hand of my righteousness.

Psalms 39:7

And now, Lord, what wait I for? my hope [is] in thee.

Mark 9:23

Jesus said unto him, If thou canst believe, all things [are] possible to him that believeth.

1 Corinthians 13:13

And now abideth faith, hope, charity, these three; but the greatest of these [is] charity.

Romans 8:24

For we are saved by hope: but hope that is seen is not hope: for what a man seeth, why doth he yet hope for?

Proverbs 23:18

For surely there is an end; and thine expectation shall not be cut off.

Proverbs 10:28

The hope of the righteous [shall be] gladness: but the expectation of the wicked shall perish.

Romans 8:25
But if we hope for that we see not, [then] do we with patience wait for [it].

Jeremiah 17:7
Blessed [is] the man that trusteth in the LORD, and whose hope the LORD is.

Psalms 71:14
But I will hope continually, and will yet praise thee more and more

Words of Appreciation

I want to thank you and the many, many persons who have purchased the Twelve Keys books. This is my twenty first published book. I am most grateful for the remarkable interest in my books. Thousands of persons have secured the books. Persons from all over the United States, Canada, Australia, New Zealand, South Korea, England, and Europe have benefited from the books.

The books have a life of their own. They find their way from person to person, from grouping to grouping by referral from friend to friend. It is amazing. Persons discover the books are helpful and refer them to their friends and family.

A friend invited me to do the annual Lectureship at his university. He was on the Faculty and had responsibility for the Lectureship. I was happy to do the Lectureship. A Consultant to Harper and Row was there. The Consultant contacted Harper and Row, strongly suggesting that they sign me to a contract for the book before some other publisher did so.

Julie and I received a contract with a generous advance. We signed the contract and wrote the book, based on my Lectures given at the university. The publishers and I thought the book would be well received in universities and graduate schools.

Twelve Keys to an Effective Church has become an extraordinary best selling book in the whole of the non-profit and church world. It is among the classic reference books in the field.

Harper and Row said to me, "Share with us what your next book is going to be." So it has gone. We are now arrived at book twenty one. It is a remarkable journey. I am most grateful for all of the persons who have contributed to this journey.

For this current book, **Living in Hope**, I am grateful to the many Persons of Hope who have blessed my life with their living examples of who hope is. It is not so much that they share "what hope is like." It is more that they teach me "who hope is." Hope comes to us in persons. Persons teach us "who hope is."

I am most deeply thankful to Julie McCoy Callahan. Her wondrous gift of hope is the primary influence in my life. We have an extraordinary life together.

For the publishing of **Living in Hope**, I am grateful to the team at CreateSpace for their excellent help. This is the third book I have had the pleasure of doing with them. I am most thankful for their assistance.

I am thankful to my many friends, family, and colleagues for their encouraging influences in my own life. Their joyful spirits, their hopeful and wondrous confidence have been extraordinary gifts in my life.

I am grateful to the people of Cuyahoga Falls, Ohio. Julie and I grew up in a wonderful town during a wonderful time. We were well blessed in our growing up years.

I am thankful for the universities that have advanced my thinking and my research. I particularly want to thank Kent State University, Southern Methodist University, and Emory University. The scholars and professors of each university have been wondrous mentors in my life.

I am grateful for all the groupings with whom I have had the privilege of speaking and consulting across the years. Their questions, insights, and suggestions have deepened my own wisdom and understanding.

I wish you well in the reading of **Living in Hope**. I pray for you a full life of hope in the years to come. God bless you.

Living in Hope

Julie

GOD BLESSES US WITH PERSONS OF HOPE.

"Ken, I want to invite you to our square dance at my church a week from this Saturday. It is the fifth Saturday in January. We always have a special event on the fifth Saturday. I invite you to come as my date. We will share a fun time."

"Thank you for the invitation. I will get back to you soon."

This was our first conversation together. We had never spoken to one another before. We had never even been introduced. We did not know one another.

In Julie's church there had been a tradition that whenever a month had a fifth Saturday, they would hold some sort of social event in the church's fellowship area on that Saturday night.

In January of 1954 the fifth Saturday's social was planned to be a square dance.

Julie and her mother always drove to the neighboring town to attend their church, and no other persons in our high school were part of their congregation.

It would be up to Julie to invite someone to be her partner during this social event.

Julie spent the winter holidays of 1953 puzzling out whether to invite someone to her church's upcoming square dance, and, if so, who?

Research included studying the high school's yearbook, looking through photos for some young man who possessed the qualities that attracted her.

A processed of elimination ensued.

Some were already "going steady" with other girls.

Others she didn't know very well.

Some she eliminated because they just didn't seem a good match.

So one day in January, as I was walking through the hallways of our high school, Julie caught my attention and stopped me.

She explained about the upcoming church social, and would I like to go with her?

We talked briefly, she shared what the social would be like, and she hoped I would like to go with her.

I said, *"Thank you for the invitation. I'll get back to you soon."*

We were standing in the hall of Cuyahoga Falls High School that morning. It was between classes.

People were rushing from one class to the next…this way and that….saying hi and hello and speaking quick messages to one another….reminding one another of get togethers, class homework, and meetings to come.

She had stopped me in the hall. Amidst the bedlam, the chaos, and the good natured fun, the joyful rushing to and fro, she stopped me in the hall.

Julie is a wondrous, remarkable person. Three amazing events happened.

The first amazing event is…. Julie spoke to me. You see, Julie was a Sophomore. I was a Senior. In that day and time, Sophomores did not speak to Seniors, unless first spoken to by the Senior. She stopped me. She spoke first. Amazing event one.

The second amazing event is….Julie invited me on a date. You see, in that day and time, girls did not invite boys on dates. It was simply not done. Granted, this event was at her church, in a nearby town, Akron, but still. Amazing event two.

I am grateful that she spoke to me and I am thankful that she invited me on this special date.

The third amazing event is that we had a grand time, a really grand time. We enjoyed being with one another, more than we might have thought we would. We talked and laughed. We had fun square dancing. We had even more fun being together. Amazing event three.

We fell in love. We dated more. We began to go steady. We became engaged. Time passed. We married.

We have been having a grand time since this wondrous square dance. Our First Date was on Saturday, January 31, 1954. This year, we celebrated the 61st Anniversary of our First Date.

We celebrated the 59th Anniversary of our Wedding on August 11, 2015.

That day, when she invited me to the square dance at her church, I thought about it. The square dance sounded like it would be fun. She sounded like she would be a wonderful date.

….Then, after we parted, I realized I did not know her name. Remember, this was the first time we had talked. It came to me that I did not know how to contact her.

I went to look for Mr. Heinz. Tall, stately, with white hair, a slow, steady walk, and a deep senatorial voice. He was the Speech teacher of the high school. He directed the class plays each spring. More importantly, for me, he was our Debate Coach for our Varsity Debate Team.

It was my custom to secure a hall pass, leave my own study hall in the school library, and go to the third floor study hall in 315 that Mr. Heinz monitored.

We would discuss our debate strategies for the coming Saturday Debate Tournament. These discussions helped greatly. We would assess the strengths of the debate teams we would be facing on Saturday, and the best ways to present a more formidable case.

Jim Coleman was my debate partner. We were an excellent team. We won an extraordinary number of debates across the state of Ohio. We were a wonderful, balanced match as a varsity debate team. Jim, to this day, can remember each debate we had and how we went about winning the debates. He has an extraordinary mind.

These conversations and strategy sessions with Mr. Heinz in his study hall were an important foundation to our success.

I knew the person who had invited me to the square dance was in Mr. Heinz's third floor study hall. I found Mr. Heinz. We made our way to his study hall. He got the seating chart out of his desk. I had noticed where she sat.

Julie McCoy

With the school directory, I was able to find her phone number, phone her, accept her kind invitation, and make arrangements for the square dance.

I learned much later that Julie, in thinking about whom to invite, had gotten out her High School Year Book. She had gone through her Sophomore class. My younger brother was in her class. She knew her class well. She studied the pictures, looking for whom to invite.

Next, she had gone through the Junior class. Many of the fellows in this class were already going with some one. There seemed to be no possibility there.

She turned to the Senior class. She found my picture.

Now, Julie had known my father when she went to Grant Elementary School. Dad was part of the Police Force of the city of

Cuyahoga Falls. For a number of years, he was in charge of the school patrols who helped elementary children across the school cross walks. She had seen him in his helping the school patrols.

And, of course, she had come to have a class acquaintanceship with my younger brother. Dan was a gifted football player. He went on to play professional football for the Cleveland Browns, the Baltimore Colts, and the New York Titans.

Julie was active in Rainbow, and she was aware that I was active in DeMolay. At the time, I was serving as Master Councilor of the Cuyahoga Falls Chapter, the second largest DeMolay Chapter in the country. The Akron Chapter, across the Cuyahoga River, was the largest Chapter.

She decided to invite me.

We had never met. We had never spoken to one another until that day in the hall between classes at Cuyahoga Falls High School.

In that time, Cuyahoga Falls was a pleasant, quiet town on the north bank of the Cuyahoga River. Akron was on the south side of the river.

The river had a steep, descending slant that made it possible to build dams and water mills to generate electricity for the rubber plants that were in Akron….Goodyear, Firestone, Goodrich, Sieberling, and many more….. In that time, all electricity was local. There was no grid. Many of the tires on the planet were made in Akron, Ohio.

Cuyahoga Falls was the nearby "bedroom" community. Many of the people who lived in Cuyahoga Falls travelled across the river to work in Akron. Julie's Dad worked for Goodyear for forty years. My Dad's Dad worked as among the first electricians for Goodyear for forty years.

When I think of Cuyahoga Falls in that time, I think of Thornton Wilder's play, "Our Town" with Emily and George. The train went through each night at the same time and most folk had retired for the night. It was a peaceful, quiet town.

Cuyahoga Falls had the High School. It had the train station, with the Doodle Bug Express and freight and passenger trains, mostly running from Columbus to Cleveland and back.

It had Water Works, built in 1936, with a wondrous swimming pool with a length of 100 meters, longer than a football field. It had four diving boards, 2 one meter boards. 1 one and one half meter board, and 1high dive, three meter board. It had a refreshment stand and a bath house. Artesian well water, brisk and cold, filled the pool. It was a gathering place of the town. I served as one of the Lifeguards there for three years.

It had Front Street. Stores and shops, eating places and groceries and the one movie theater in town. On a Saturday, we would walk from our home on Myrtle Avenue to the movie theater on Front Street. We would watch the news feature, the cliff hanging serial, the cartoons, usually three cartoons, and two major feature movies.

Next to the movie theater was the new supermarket, run by my Dad. There had been four corner grocery stores in the town. Dad's idea was to have one large store with a better selection of foods and meats. His new store fed the town through the depression. It was a major gathering place.

There was a dedicated block of churches up from Front Street, between Second Street and Third Street, one on each corner of the block. Many worship services, many weddings, and many funerals took place on that block.

Scattered across the town, there were parks and ball fields. Oak Park was a special place, with its small pool, clay tennis courts, playground equipment, and fields for neighborhood baseball and football. The Rowena Ross Park was in honor of Julie's cousin who was the first woman to die in World War II. She fell ill in Hollandia, near New Guinea, and quickly passed away.

Cuyahoga Falls had State Road, with its range of newer shops and businesses, drive in eateries, and our first shopping mall at the corner of Portage Trail and State Road. There was much excitement as it was being built.

We had the Soap Box Derby near by in Akron.

We had the Gorge. The Cuyahoga River created the Cuyahoga Gorge. The Cuyahoga Indians were ancient dwellers in the Gorge. There was the Old Maid's Kitchen, a large cave with a strong history.

I have fond memories of many joyful adventures in the Gorge. Richard Barr and I were close friends and we had many explorations along the paths and trails, in the caves and dens, and up and down the rocks and chasms. We climbed the underside of the High Level Bridge that linked Cuyahoga Falls and Akron. We waded in and swam in the Cuyahoga River.

The Gorge was our happy adventure ground.

I learned later that Julie and Sue Swain, her good friend, enjoyed many exploration adventures in the Gorge. Sue's home was actually on Highbridge Trail at the edge of the Gorge. Julie and Sue would gather at Sue's home and head out for an adventure in the Gorge.

Julie and I grew up in a good time. Cuyahoga Falls was good people, and a good town.

We weathered the wars. My Dad fought in the War in the Pacific. My Uncle fought in the war in North Africa and Europe. We call this World War II. My wisdom is that it really was two major wars fought in very distinctive ways. We came back from these two wars and tried to take up life again.

Julie's Dad had fought in the Great War; what we now call World War I. It was a bloody war of trenches and barb wire, retreats and advances, mud and death. Julie's brother fought in the Korean War. These wars disrupted life in Cuyahoga Falls in tough, devastating ways.

And, as best we could, the town tried to continue on its peaceful, quiet way of life, with tree lined Broad Boulevard with its dividing strip of grasses, flowers, and trees, its elementary schools, two junior high schools, and its one high school.

It was here, at Cuyahoga Falls High School, that Julie and I came to meet. Her invitation to a square dance at her church began our life together.

Much has happened since that eventful night....

This wisdom has come to me in the time come and gone.

God blesses us with Persons of Hope.

Julie is a Person of Hope. With Julie, I discover, each day, what it is like to live in hope.

God sends to us Persons of Hope so that we have living examples of what it is like to live in hope. God senses that we experience hope in persons more than we do in logic or prose, treatises and soliloquies, poems and songs, and learned dissertations. All of these resources help.

Persons of hope help us to discover hope best. God sends us living examples of hope. Hope comes in a person. The person is the description of hope. The person is hope.

Julie is a person of grace and compassion. She has the gifts of peace and calm. Most especially, she lives a life of hope and encouragement.

I learn, each day, from her gift of hope.

You are welcome to consider the persons in your life who are Persons of Hope with you. Share much time with these persons. Remember these persons in your feelings and thoughts. Feel free to make a list of these persons and the ways they bless your life.

Secure your list on your mirror, in your car, in your computer, your kitchen, your workshop, your desk, and wherever will help you to sense the presence of the Persons of Hope with which God blesses your life. From time to time, look at your list. Remember well the Persons of Hope who influence and shape your life.

A Person of Hope is an encouraging person, a person who looks toward the best in people, who sees their strengths, gifts, and competencies. A Person of Hope is a person with confidence and assurance, a constructive, positive spirit, a person who looks to the best in persons and in life.

Some persons, a few, are persons with wishful thinking. This is not hope. Some persons are sad, angry, and depressed. This is not hope. Some want to develop dependent and co-dependent patterns of behavior. This is not hope. Some persons are weak and wimpy, and they talk much of hope. None of these are Persons of Hope.

Now, they may drift into talk of hope as the antidote to their difficulties. Talking about hope is different from living in hope.

God blesses you with Persons of Hope, who quietly and gently, live lives of hope, with a spirit of grace and peace.

I am amazed at the many, many Persons of Hope with whom God blesses my life.

Julie is the most significant, and, across the years, many more have come into my life. When I think of hope, I think of all of these persons and what they have taught me about the nature and spirit of hope.

A possibility for understanding the amazing gift of hope is to discover all of the Persons of Hope with whom God blesses your life. Reflect on these persons. Be in prayer about them. Discuss them with a few close friends. Claim the Persons of Hope in your life. Spend much time with the Persons of Hope present in your life.

Living in hope is discovering the Persons of Hope with whom God blesses you.

Mrs. Lott

GOD ENCOURAGES US TO DISCOVER PERSONS OF HOPE.

"Dr. Callahan, please help us find a pastor who will come to love us, and whom we can come to love, and who will bring us hope."

Mrs. Lott and I were standing on the front porch stoop of her Piney Grove church. She and I were there visiting after the worship service of that Sunday morning. Most people had gone. It hadn't taken that long. There weren't that many people to have left.

It was a wonderful fall day, with the leaves turning and the color emerging on the trees. A gentle breeze gave a quiet coolness to the air. It was a special day.

We had had a good worship service. The pastor of the moment had shared a solid sermon. The pastor was moving on. The following spring he was headed to the mission field across the planet.

Mrs. Lott was not just looking for hope for her church. She was looking for hope for her life.

Her husband had retired from the farm, rattling around the old farm house, day to day, not quite sure what to do from one day to the next. His life had been the farm, the tiling of the soil, the planting of the seed, the raising of the crops, the caring for the animals, the seasons of the farm. All that was gone. He could see no future.

Mrs. Lott shared with me about her family. She was married after the Great War. Raising six children. Living all her life on the farm. Going to the distant village now and then, for supplies. Her family now scattered asunder, across the landscape of North America. Mostly, doing all right. Now, her mother was in her nineties. In a nearby nursing home. Slowly dying of cancer. No hope.

Mrs. Lott shared about the strange, new people who had moved in, up and down Flowery Springs Road. They stayed up past ten o'clock at night. They wore clothes she had never seen before. They were noisy in their living. Slamming car doors. Banging on this or that. Noisy. Loud, laughing, carrying on. They went to town a lot. They were, best she could tell, really city folk at heart.

What with her husband and her mother and these strange new people, she was having trouble seeing hope in her life. She was saying that the sources of hope that had been working for her for years upon years were no longer working for her. She could see no hope.

Well, perhaps. Mrs. Lott went on to say, "Dr. Callahan, I want you to know that I do everything that I now do based on whether it will help me be part of God's Kingdom in the next life. I don't see any hope in this life. I once did. My hope is now for the next life."

I knew, as she shared these words, that Mrs. Lott was not living in the past. She was living in the next life future, beyond the River. She was asking for a pastor who could help her discover new sources of hope for her present, immediate future, and distant future.

She had not quite given up.... on hope for her life now.

I noted her longing for a pastor who could come and love them, whom they could come to love, and who would help them discover sources of hope for now. She was looking for a pastor who could love them, not lead them. She was looking for a pastor who could help her find hope for her life, not her church. Her deeper longing and yearning was to discover sources of hope for all of life, more than simply church life

I noted her association of love and hope. Love and hope are good friends. They go together. When we find love, we find hope. Love and hope are good friends.

When we search for hope, we search for love. When we find one, we find both.... hope and love. Grace, compassion, and love are good friends with our hope for the present, the immediate future, the distant future, and the next life future.

Mrs. Lott had postponed her hopes,....almost, to the next life future. She had,....almost, become a part of the River People.

Yes, and sometimes, we are the Flimsies People. We focus our sources of hope on the Flimsies of this life. The new car, the new clothes, the new this or that.... until it gets its first dent or tear.

Sometimes, you and I are the Cliff People. We find ourselves frozen on the face of a cliff, with no hand holds or foot holds ahead, and we can no longer reach the hand holds or foot holds behind. We freeze, and clutch and cling and hold on for dear life. We want no change. The only change we can see is the abyss below.

Sometimes, we are the River People. Sometimes, we are the Flimsies People. Sometimes, we are the Cliff People.

When we live life at our best, we are the Easter people. We life in hope for the Present, the Immediate Future, the Distant Future, and the Next Life Future.

We live in the hope God gives us. We live in the hope with which God blesses us. God blesses us with hope for this life, and for the life to come.

We live in grace, peace, and hope, not to earn our future or merit it by kind and noble deeds, striving to earn what we have already been given. We live in grace, peace, and hope in humble gratitude that our present and our future have already been given to us. We live with the confidence, the assurance that these sources of hope are not of our own doings, graspings, and clutchings.

We live, knowing that we are the People of the Manger, the People of the Supper, the People of Easter. We live in the confidence and assurance that we are the people of the open tomb, the risen Lord, and new life in Christ. We live in hope.

Hope gathers up the sacrament of the coming of grace in the manger, the sacrament of the coming of peace in the supper, and the sacrament of the coming of hope in the open tomb. Hope gathers grace and peace. Living in grace and living in peace, we live in hope.

Hope is the confidence and assurance that the present and the future are secure and promising. We know there will be bumps and bruises, failures and defeat, despair and depression. Even so, we live secure in the grace of God, the peace of Christ, and the hope of the Holy Spirit. We live in the promise of grace, peace, and hope.

God encourages us to discover Persons of Hope. Thus, we actively search for Persons of Hope.

I sometimes say to a person, "Share with me where you were born, and what has happened since." Or, I may say, "Share with me what you have fun doing." Or, I may invite, "Share with me about yourself." I am inviting them to teach me who they are and the spirit with which they live life. I am encouraging them to share the extent to which they are a Person of Hope.

A possibility for coming to understand the gift of hope is to actively seek out new Persons of Hope who will bless your life. Look for, intentionally and purposefully, these new Persons of Hope who will bless and enrich your life. Claim these new Persons of Hope in your life. Spend much time with these new Persons of Hope present now in your life.

Living in hope is seeking new Persons of Hope with whom God blesses you.

It is amazing to me that when we look for Persons of Hope we find them. What we look for is often what we find. Were we to go looking for persons who are worried or anxious, troubled or depressed we might likely find them as well.

To live life as a Person of Hope, discover, look for, and search out new Persons of Hope. **Who you look for is who you become.**

You

GOD INVITES US TO BE PERSONS OF HOPE.

God invites you to be a Person of Hope. Live you. Live your search for hope. You will live in hope.

Live you as in the self who is easy-going, enjoyable, likeable, and interested in other people. You are not you, really you, when you are tense, tight, nervous, anxious, angry, upset, and on and on. Yes, all of those ingredients are a part of you. You are the whole you.

And, you are really you when you live beyond those things that so weigh you down. The things that weigh you down, the "weighing downs," are the tense, tight, nervous, anxious, fear, anxieties, angry, rage, upset, depressing, despairing, gloomy, glum, insecurities of the moment, and on and on.

Mostly, when you are drawn to those "weighing downs," you are drawn to things that are not really you. What draws us to those weights is our misguided efforts to be some one we really are not. When you seek to be someone else, you are not you. In seeking to be someone else, you loose hope.

God blesses you with you and the hope that comes with being you. When you try to be someone else, you may gain "whatever hope they may have," but you loose the hope God has vested in you.

Live you. No one but you can live you. Be yourself. Be not codependent. Be not disturbingly dependent on other persons. Dependency robs you of the ability to be yourself.

Live you as a selfless you, not a selfish you. *Live you* does not mean to live as a selfish, preoccupied, self-serving person. When you are a selfish you, you are not you.

Persons who are selfish are not really selfish. Oh, a few may be.

Mostly, when you find a selfish person you have found a person who is scared or scarred…. or both. They are using their selfishness as a self protective mechanism so as to not be scared or scarred yet again. The person who is conserving and holding, protecting and preserving is really hoping (hear the word) to not be yet again scared or scarred.

We are whole beings, whole persons. We are beings of the heart, emotional beings, who love and laugh, share compassion, feel joy and sorrow, experience fear and anger, guilt and forgiveness.

We are beings of the community, belonging beings, who long for roots, place, belonging, friends, family. We are beings of the mind, intellectual beings, who think and reflect, ponder and consider, discover and create; we search for meaning and purpose in our lives.

We are beings of the will, willful beings, who have a sense of will and direction, purpose and focus, determination and resolution; we seek to move forward in our lives. We are beings of hope, spiritual beings, with yearnings and longings, strivings and aspirations, confidences and assurances, vision and hope, who search for that which is holy and sacred in this life and the next.

We are physical beings, who breathe and move, walk and run, lift and carry, hunger and thirst, sleep and wake. We enjoy good health and well-being, and then illness and sickness may come to us. We care for, look after, and nourish our physical body.

We are more than our body and we are our body. We cannot live this life apart from our body. We are whole beings in our heart, longings, mind, will, spirit, and body. God invites us to develop a healthy, hope filled heart, longing, minds, will, spirit, and body – to have an encouraging, constructive, positive approach about our whole being.

We accept graciously, gratefully, thankfully the gift of life. We treasure this priceless gift. We are generous, good stewards of it. We see the precious gift for what it is. It is not that we hoard it.

We receive the gift of life with awe and appreciation, wonder and joy. We grow and advance the gift of life with which God has blessed us. Likewise, we receive the gift of our heart, longing, mind, will, spirit, and body with awe and appreciation. We grow and advance these wonderful gifts of God.

We are given these precious gifts for this lifetime. These gifts are the sacraments, the outward and visible signs of the inner and invisible grace, creativity, and creation of God. These gifts are the signs of grace, compassion, community, and hope. These gifts are the tangible signs of God's love and grace with us. God gives us these gifts that we might live in this life.

You are your future. You are who you love. You are who you belong with. You are who you think. You are who you will to be. You are who you hope for.

What you do with *you* shapes your future. Emerging trends rise and fall. Some things come and go. Good surprises come your way. Tragic events darken your life. Sinful events weigh you down. Take their toll. Anxiety and anger visit you. Doubt and disbelief come to you.

Good fun and good times bless your life. Wonder and joy are your friends. Grace and compassion surround you. Peace comforts you. Hope leads you. Amidst all of these gifts and happenings, how you relate to these events shapes your future.

We are living on the threshold of a new age of hope in the history of humankind. It is what you do with this new time that gives you your future.

It is how you grow you that is decisive. You can grow you. You can control you.

You cannot control the events and people around you. You can control how you relate to the events and persons in your life. Events swirl, swiftly and suddenly. People do this, and then they do that. They are less than predictable. Amidst the changes that abound, you can control you. Have this confidence and assurance.

> Grace is stronger than law.
> > We are the people of grace.
> Compassion is stronger than legalism.
> > We are the people of compassion.
> Easter is stronger than Good Friday.
> > We are the Easter people.
> The open tomb is stronger than the bloodied cross.
> > We are the people of the open tomb.
> The Risen Lord is stronger than the dead Jesus.
> > We are the people of the Risen Lord.
> We are the resurrection people.
> > We are the people of hope.
> Know the grace and mercy of God,
> > the peace and calm of Christ,
> > > the hope and encouragement of the Holy Spirit.
> Claim the Persons of Hope with whom God blesses you.

Search for new Persons of Hope.

Be a Person of Hope.

Gather your mentors around you.

Do many one-time events to grow you.

You are your future.

Live your search. You will live in hope.

Life is a search. Life is a pilgrimage. Live your search.

You will live in hope.

Your search is your hope. Your hope is your search.

We search and we discover hope. We hope and we discover our search.

Hope is in the search more than in the finding. And, in the searching, we find.

In life, we make our fair share of mistakes. Some are simple mistakes. Some are excellent mistakes. Sometimes, we make more excellent mistakes than we wish. Some are most grievous mistakes. Sometimes, we learn from our mistakes. Sometimes, we learn just enough from our mistakes that we can move on in our search.

Life is peace and panic, fear and release, qualms and quiet, fear and anxiety, calmness and conflict, forgiving and reconciling, tears and compassion, worry and quietness, tragedy and wonder, sorrow and cheer, old ways and new discoveries, doubt and death, hope and new ways. Life gives us a range of experiences: honest and horrific, humorous and holy.

Life is laughter and sadness, joy and despair, good times and dark tragedy, faith and fright, a mingling of confidence and assurance, doubt and dread, security and fright, serenity and bravery.

Life is birthday parties and toothaches, birds singing and dark storms. Life is joyous laughter and solemn funerals. Life is happiness and sadness, awe and humility, jealousy and generosity.

There are moments of accomplishment and achievement. There are flashes of dusky rage and raw terror. There are times of passive-aggressive behavior, low-grade hostility, subliminal resentment, and eruptive forms of anger.

There are events of wonder and joy, new life and hope. There are times when we feel the lowest of the lowest, and there are times we mount like eagles to the heavens.

Life is simple. Life is complex. It is now one thing, and then it is another. There are good surprises, cheerful moments, deep passion, and great love. There are moments when we are brimming over with joy. There are times of confusion and retreat.

Life has its quiet times, peaceful and tranquil, and its noisy, boisterous times. There are harsh, hard times, and pleasant, delightful times. We are awkward and anxious. We are upset and afraid.

We discover excellent ideas and good suggestions. We have questions and puzzlements. There are moments of promise and faith. There are confident times of assurance and hope.

We move forward and slide backward. Progress is our friend. Defeat overtakes us. Power and hope join us. Defeat and tragedy do us in. Sorrow and grief abide with us. Grace and hope and love lead us.

We are children. We are adults. We are something in between. We act graciously, and thoughtlessly. We act with consideration, and with haste. We gossip too much, and we are politely silent.

We are careless and neglectful. Foolish and irrational. Impulsive and awkward. Generous and giving. Scared and scarred. Selfish and stingy. Timid and cautious. Brave and bold. We live in fear. We do courageous deeds. We are creative. We discover.

Death haunts us. Resurrection is our hope.

We long for the habits that encourage us to be highly helpful people. We discover life is not as simple as seven habits for highly effective people. Sometimes, we are effective. Sometimes, we are not. We do want our life to count, to be helpful.

God invites us to a life of service, not a life of survival. God encourages us to the enduring sacraments of grace and compassion, peace and calm, hope and confidence, not to the frail altar of worldly success, anxiety and doubt, false feats and dubious enterprises.

Life is a search.

We are drawn to movements that help us fulfill, for this time, our deepest yearnings and longings, our foundational life searches.

We search for individuality....for identity, integrity, autonomy, and power. Amidst the powerlessness of our times, we search for the sense of having some stake, some control over our own lives and destinies.

We search for community....for roots, place, belonging, sharing and caring, friends and family. We long for home. We sense the joy in the thought that there is no place like home. Yes, we know of homes filled with shouting and pouting, anger and bitterness, betrayal and resentment. And, we long for a home filled with grace and compassion, peace and calm, love and hope.

We search for meaning.... for purpose and understanding, value and significance in every day, ordinary life. We long for some sense to life. We do not yearn for high and lofty schemes, or for abstract and complex eruditions of life. We hope for the sense of purpose for our lives and some understanding of what life is about.

We search for hope....for some confidence and assurance for the present, the immediate future, the distant future, and the next life future beyond the River.

In the end, our search leads us to the discovery that success is service. The fleeting flimsies of this life come and go, wither and vanish. What remains, what endures are acts of grace and compassion, moments of peace and calm, events of community and kindness, the sharing of service and hope.

A possibility for understanding the gift of hope is to actively be a Person of Hope who blesses the lives of many persons. Feel free to live life as a Person of Hope. Be, intentionally and purposefully, a Person of Hope who will bless and enrich the lives of many persons. Ask yourself, at any given moment, am I behaving as a Person of Hope.

Living in hope is being a Person of Hope. God blesses you to be this Person.

Everything done in human kind is done on hope.

More fully, everything done in the universe is done on hope. The universe begins in hope. Hope is not at the end of life only.

Hope is present before the beginning of the universe.

Hope begins the universe. Hope is the beginning of life. The beginning of the universe is an act of hope, a stirring of hope for the universe to come.

Hope is not only on the other side of the river. Hope is before the beginning act that brings the whole of the universe into being. Before the universe was born, there was hope, there was God. Before you were born, there was hope.

You can count on three realities. God blesses us with Persons of Hope. God encourages us to discover Persons of Hope. God invites you to be a Person of Hope.

God blesses us with Persons of Hope.
God encourages us to discover new Persons of Hope.
God invites us to be Persons of Hope.

Strengths

GOD BLESSES US WITH STRENGTHS.

God blesses you with your strengths. Your strengths are sources of Hope. Live your strengths. You will live in hope. When you live your weaknesses, you will live in despair.

It is natural to play to your strengths. Where ever you are, claim your strengths, build on your strengths, and do better what you do best.

When you are on a basket ball court, and your strengths are football strengths, play to your football strengths.

I had coached our church basketball team for four years. At the end of the four years, I said to my guys, "No more. I cannot coach any more."

Those of you involved in coaching know the investment of time it takes each week; the Tuesday night practice, the Thursday night practice, scouting the other teams, and playing the game on Saturday.

My schedule of teaching, research, writing, speaking, and consulting had become so complicated around the country and across the world that some things had to give way. So I said to my guys, "It's been a grand four years, but I can't do it anymore."

My guys said to me,

"Coach, we're all going to be seniors in high school this coming year. Coach us one more year."

That was a plaintive plea. We had been good family with one another. We were a good team. I wondered, "Could I do it one more year?"

Julie and I talked. It occurred to us that I might find time to do a Thursday night practice and coach the games on Saturday. There would be no Tuesday night practice. There would be no scouting other teams. On that basis, I said to my guys, "I'll coach one more year."

I was wise enough to know that, if halfway through the season we were not winning our fair share of games; my guys would be back at me. We would end up with a Tuesday night practice, a make-up Wednesday night practice, more scouting of the other teams, and playing the games on Saturday. I would be involved even more intensely and extensively than before.

I thought, what do we have going for us that will help us, with one practice and no scouting, to do as well as we have in our previous four seasons?

It had been sitting in front of me for four years. I had not seen it. My guys were the best *football* team in the county.

Since seventh grade, they had been in spring football practices, illegal summer football practices, and the legal summer practices. They had played football all season long. They came to me, each year, at the start of basketball season, as the best football players in the county.

So, in the first Thursday practice, I said to my guys, "This season there are three steps to our offense and our defense. Here is our basket. Sometimes, when we shoot at our basket and miss, someone on the other team is unfortunate enough, unlucky enough to get the rebound.

"Step one: I want the two of you who are nearest him to converge on him as though he were a quarterback seeking to throw a long pass down field. Intimidate him, terrify him, and help him know that his life's future – and that of his children and grandchildren – rests on his lateraling sideways. Any attempt downfield puts his future in considerable jeopardy.

"Step two: That gives the other three of you time to set up our secondary zone pass defense, like you learned to run in seventh grade football and have run every year since. The half-court mark of the basketball court is now the fifty-yard line. Set up on our side of the fifty-yard line.

"Step three: Intercept the second pass downfield, drive for the basket, make the lay-up, and turn right around and do the same three steps again, as they *try* to throw it in from out of bounds.

"This court is now our football field. We are no longer going to go meekly, mildly clear down to the other end of the field and set up a basketball two-one-two zone defense we haven't figured out to run in four years anyway. We are going to play as much of the game as possible in our end of the field."

My guys liked this approach to the game. It matched with their strengths. They rose to it. They loved it. They thrived on it.

There is one problem with this approach to the game. It is spelled ***fouls***.

I was much embarrassed during the third game of the season when one of my guys fouled out before half-time. I was even more embarrassed when, as he came to the bench, my bench cleared itself and welcomed him as though he were some kind of conquering hero. I was even more embarrassed because our stands were cheering.

From that game on, whenever a foul was called on one of my team, my bench and our stands cheered. The other coaches would look down the way and shake their heads, wondering what we were doing.

Each Thursday practice I said to my guys, "Give up the cross-body blocks. Quit tackling their players. We don't touch them. We don't tackle them. In that sense, this is basketball. We simply terrify and intimidate them. We force them to lateral the ball. We intercept that second pass, drive to the basket, make the lay-up, and turn right around and do it again as they try to throw the ball in. We play to our strengths."

"We do not touch them."

The last game of the season, we got to play the goliaths of the league. They never practiced. They played in three other leagues. They played basketball the whole week long. I'm convinced they never had their tennis shoes off once during the whole season. If you stood downwind from them, you would know what I mean.

So here we were, with five minutes remaining in the fourth quarter, and all my guys except three had fouled out.

It was in that game I learned you could finish a game with however many were left. I had always known the rule that you had to have five to start a game. But, in that game I learned, in the rules of that particular league, you could finish with however many players were left.

I began to wonder, "Now, when we get down to one, how does he pass the ball in to himself from out of bounds?"

We finished the last five minutes of the fourth quarter, playing three of our players against the five goliaths of the league. We beat that team 71 to 63.

Their coach had not prepared them for us. They had never seen basketball played the way we played the game. We had three steps. We consistently did those three steps. We played the game the way we could play best.

When the game was over, we ended up a writhing mass of humanity on the floor, hugging and carrying on. More injuries occur at that point in a game than any other.

We finally gathered ourselves from the floor and were standing around cheering and carrying on in a circle. My guys said to me, "Coach, we're all going away to college this coming year, but we'll all come home on Saturday, if you'll *coach us one more year.*"

In that one season, my guys played their best. They contributed more speed, quickness, teamwork, energy, and perspiration than all four previous seasons together. They played each game to their fullest, and then some. Their attitude, their actions, their accomplishments were amazing to behold. They were building on their strengths, doing what they knew how to do best.

I learned an important lesson in life that season.

When we look for the strengths we wish we had, we miss the strengths we really have.

I had spent four years looking for basketball strengths. I had missed the strengths we really had – football strengths.

The art is to build on the strengths you really have, not the ones you wish you had.

Look for the strengths you really have. When you look for the strengths you really have, you *find* the strengths you really have. Build on them. Expand one of them. You grow richer, fuller strengths along the way.

If you look for the strengths you wish you had, you miss the strengths you already have. Claim your strengths. Expand one of your current strengths.

Be less preoccupied with any weakness you may have. Be more occupied with the strengths you have. When you claim your strengths, you claim God's gifts. When you deny, pay less attention to, your strengths, you deny God's gifts. You deny God.

God gives you your strengths so you can claim them, build on them, and grow forward. In a subtle way, becoming preoccupied with your weaknesses is the Devil's way of distracting you from your strengths.

Life Strengths.

What is true for basketball strengths is true for Life Strengths. In my book, *Twelve Strengths for Living*, you discover the key strengths of living a whole, healthy life in the grace of God. Claim the strengths God gives to you. Build on them. Have fun growing them. Live more fully on them. Let these strengths be for you a source of hope.

Vocational Strengths.

What is true for basketball is true also for vocational strengths. Mary's mother had always wanted Mary to be a teacher....because her mother had always wanted to be a teacher and never did. With her mother's persistent and irksome nagging, Mary studied at the university to be a teacher, graduated with a teaching degree, and became a teacher.

She taught for ten years, and did reasonably well. For herself, Mary had always wanted to be a nurse. She had the confidence that her real strengths were in nursing. She went to nursing school and graduated with honors. She has been a nurse, happily and contented, now for eight years. She is living her vocational strengths.

John loved woodworking, building furniture, making art pieces in wood. He practiced his love through the university, law school, and an advanced degree. He practiced law, most successfully. And, he finally gave up his law practice for his real love, his woodworking. He said to me, "Life is short. I am a good lawyer. I am a better woodworker. This is where my real strengths are. This is where my real love is.

Mary and John are two of countless persons I have had the honor of knowing across the years who have found their vocational strengths, and live in hope.

Motivational Strengths.

I will share about motivational strengths in the next chapter.

Relational – Achievement Strengths.

Some persons are excellent in relations and some persons are extraordinary in achievements. Some do both well. For many persons, their strengths are in relationships. They thrive in developing friendships. They love roots, place, belonging, friends, and family. For them, life is community. Having close friends and family is success in life.

Michael came home from school one day. I said, "How did school go today." Michael said, "Great, Dad. I made four new friends." For Michael, school is community. School is friendship. How he had done on the algebra text was somewhat beside the point.

Michael is our youngest son. He is the only one who has had to learn how to get along with three other people - his older brother, mother, and father. He has wonderful friendship, community strengths.

For many persons, their strengths are in achievements, accomplishments, goals, and objectives. They measure success by what they achieve. They have a driving passion to accomplish specific objectives. They do. Their strength is functional and operational.

Yes, some persons have both relational-friendship strengths and functional-achievement strengths.

The art is to build on the strengths you really have. You will live in hope.

Joy, Laughter, and Fun Strengths.

Many persons have the gifts, strengths, and competencies of having the strengths of joy, laughter, and fun. These persons enjoy the fun of life. For them, life is not sad and dreary, despondent and despairing. For them, life is wonder and joy, good fun and good times. They reveal in the wondrous and extraordinary gift of the life God has given to them.

We are encouraged to live life as a great banquet of God's grace, as a wedding feast of God's hope. Grim and glum are not the marks of a healthy life. Yes, there are moments of pain and distress, darkness and despair. And, life has much to do with joy and laughter, good fun and good times.

Economic, Cultural, Social Strengths.

God blesses us with economic, cultural, and social strengths for a whole, healthy life. We live with these three as good friends. They go together. You cannot separate one from the other. The economic and the cultural intermix. The cultural and the social come together with one another. All three are a dynamic mix with one another,

Grace, Peace, Hope.

Grace, Peace, and Hope are the strongest strengths of all. The Grace of God, the Peace of Christ, and the Hope of the Holy Spirit are the most extraordinary gifts with which God blesses us. We are, finally, who we really are in the gifts of grace, peace, and hope with which God blesses us.

God blesses you with these Strengths
>   Life Strengths.
>   Vocational Strengths.
>   Motivational Strengths.
>   Relational – Achievement Strengths.
>   Joy, Laughter, and Fun Strengths.
>   Economic, Cultural, Social Strengths.
>   Grace, Peace, Hope Strengths.

Focus on your strongest strength, not your weakest weakness. To focus on your weakest weakness is to decide to live with no hope. God gives you your strengths so you can live in hope. Claim your strengths. You will live in hope.

You can count on four realities. God blesses us with Persons of Hope. God encourages us to discover Persons of Hope. God invites you to be a Person of Hope. God blesses you with strengths.

A possibility for coming to understand the gift of hope is to actively claim the strengths with which God blesses you. Feel free to claim your strengths. Build on your strengths. When we focus on a weakness, we live in despair. Expand a current strength. Do better what you do best.

Build on your strengths. Live in hope.
Living in hope is building on your strengths.

Motivations

GOD BLESSES US WITH MOTIVATIONS.

God blesses you with your motivations. Your primary motivations are sources of hope. Live your major motivations. You will live in hope. When you live your lesser motivations, you will live in despair. When you live someone else's motivations, you will live in despair and depression. When you live your own motivations, you live in hope.

Motivation is internal.

People internally motivate themselves toward objectives for which they have ownership. People are glad to motivate themselves forward. They are happy to self-motivate themselves. They accomplish and achieve objectives that match with their own primary motivations.

Motivation is a match.

A motivational match is where the grassroots and the key leaders of a given grouping have achieved a match on the same motivational wave length. For example, the grassroots of a grouping motivate themselves on the motivation of compassion and the key leaders of the grouping motivate themselves on the same motivational wave length of compassion.

This is a motivational match. Because of this motivational match, the whole grouping, grassroots and key leaders, moves forward together. There is a sense of a common focus of motivation. There is a sense of a common language of motivation. Grassroots and key leaders are on the same motivational wave length.

Because of this motivational match, many people pitch in and help, generous giving happens, and the whole grouping has good fun and good times as they achieve the project together. Grassroots and key leaders have deep satisfaction because of their common motivational wave length.

Motivation can be a motivational gap.

A grouping of grassroots and key leaders could suffer from a motivational gap.

The grassroots motivate themselves on one motivation and the key leaders motivate themselves on another motivation.

For example, the grassroots motivate themselves on the motivation of compassion and the key leaders motivate themselves on the motivation of challenge. There is no match. There is a motivational gap. The result is that the key leaders do most of the work and give most of the money. The same few people move a project forward.

Manipulation is external.

In some groupings, the key leaders insist that their primary motivation be the dominate motivation for the whole grouping. They do not listen to the primary motivation of the grassroots. The result is an effort at manipulation by the key leaders.

Motivation becomes manipulation when the key leaders try to superimpose their motivation on the grassroots. Such an external super imposition comes across to the grassroots as manipulation.

It is.

People are less willing to motivate themselves toward objectives out of someone else's motivations. When the motivations come from someone else, people tend not to motivate themselves to move toward the objectives.

Six Primary Motivations

God blesses us with six primary motivations. All six are present within you. You can grow forward any of the six you would have fun growing and developing. You are not locked into a specific major motivation.

Compassion

One of life's major motivations is compassion – grace, forgiving, sharing, caring, giving, loving, and serving. Many persons do what they do out of the motivation of compassion.

Community

Many persons do what they do out of the motivation of community – roots, place, belonging, good fun, and good times. For them, the primary motivation is family and friends. They do what they do because family and belonging are central motivations in their lives.

Hope

One of life's major motivations is hope. Every thing done in human kind is done on hope. We long for hope in the present, the immediate future, the distant future, and the next life future beyond the River. We yearn for some confidence and assurance for the present and for the future.

Challenge

One of life's major motivations is challenge. The motivation is one of achievement and attainment and accomplishment. Persons look forward to rising to challenge, to achieving the result. The goal is attaining the result.

Reasonability

One of life's major motivations is reasonability. The motivation is one of data, analysis, logic, and it makes good sense.

Commitment

One of life's major motivations is commitment. Duty, vow, obligation, and loyalty are central to the motivation of commitment.

One or two of the six may be predominate at a given point in your life's pilgrimage. At another point in your life, it may be yet another one or two that are predominate.

Momentum begins with motivation. Motivations stir momentum. Strong, healthy groupings create a motivational match.

The major motivations present in persons and in groupings are:

>Compassion,
>Community,
>Hope,
>Challenge,
>Reasonability,
>Commitment.

Frequently, I refer to these as motivational resources. Motivation is internal, not external. These are the constructive motivational resources inside a person with which persons motivates themselves forward.

All six are present in every person. God blesses every person with all six. You can grow any of the motivations forward in your life. For a variety of reasons, people tend to have grown forward one or two as their primary motivations for this time of life. Life is a pilgrimage. Life is a search. At another stage of life, you might grow forward another one or two of the motivational resources

A Motivational Match with Congregations

I am with many congregations who say to me, "Dr. Callahan, we want you to know our worship attendance is strong, many people attend, many people do most of the work, and many people give generously." I immediately know I am with congregations who have a motivational match.

Congregations with a strong track record of action, implementation, and momentum have an excellent match of motivational resources between key leaders, the pastor and staff, the grass roots in the congregation, and the unchurched in the community.

The motivational match happens whenever the key leaders, grassroots, pastor/staff, and unchurched find a motivational match….a common motivational resonance with two of these three:

Compassion
Community
Hope

We do not need resonance on all three. We will have strong momentum when we have a match on any two of the three. A match occurs when two of these are the prevailing motivational resources in the congregation. There is a strong sense of continuity, reliability, and stability in the congregation. There is a healthy spirit of momentum. We act swiftly.

A strong, healthy congregation develops a strong motivational match between the key leaders, the grass roots, the pastor/staff, and the unchurched. A weak, declining congregation creates a motivational gap. A dying congregation makes the motivational gap wider.

With the following chart, you can see which two major motivations are present with the key leaders, grassroots, pastor and staff, and the unchurched in the community. In this fashion you can discover whether you have a motivational match or a motivational gap.

A Motivational Match in Strong, Healthy Congregations

	Key Leaders	Grass Roots	Pastor Staff	Un churched
Compassion	X	X	X	X
Community	X	X	X	X
Hope				
Challenge				
Reasonability				
Commitment				

Compassion — sharing, caring, giving, loving, serving

Community — good fun, good times, belonging, family

Hope — confidence, assurance in the grace of God

Challenge — accomplishment, achievement, attainment

Reasonability — data, analysis, logic, it makes good sense

Commitment — duty, vow, obligation, loyalty

A Motivational Gap in Weak, Declining and Dying Congregations

	Key Leaders	Grass Roots	Pastor Staff	Un churched
Compassion		X		X
Community		X		X
Hope				
Challenge	X		X	
Reasonability				
Commitment	X		X	

A Motivational Gap with Congregations

I am with many congregations who say to me, "Dr. Callahan, we want you to know our worship attendance is meager, the same few people attend, the same few people do most of the work, and the same few people give most of the money." I immediately know I am with congregations who have a motivational gap. Wherever there is a mismatch of motivational resources, there is a weak or nonexistent track record of implementation.

I share this suggestion with both the key leaders and the pastor: "You want to bridge from your predominant motivational resources to those that are present among the grass roots. Then, you will motivate and mobilize the strengths, gifts, competencies, and financial resources of the grass roots. You will mobilize the grace, peace, and hope of the whole congregation."

The way forward is to **bridge** the motivational resources to create a helpful match.

Frequently, the reason some things do not happen in a local congregation is because what motivates the key leaders and the pastor differs from what motivates the grass roots of the congregation, and does not resonate with the unchurched in the community.

The keys leaders and the pastor share the same motivational resources, but the grass roots motivate themselves out of different motivational resources. They do not resonate well….fit well together.

There is a "motivational gap." Note….it is not a commitment gap. Sometimes, that is what pastors and key leaders mistakenly conclude, particularly as they tend to work out of the motivational resource of commitment.

In a motivational gap, the key leaders and pastor broadcast on the radio wave links of challenge and commitment. The grassroots and the unchurched have their radios tuned to compassion and community. There is no resonance. There is no match. It is a motivational gap.

In committee meeting after committee meeting, the key leaders and the pastor say to one another, "If people were only more committed and would rise to the challenge, this blooming venture would get better." The hook, the catch is the grassroots and the unchurched do not motivate themselves in high challenge, deeply committed ways.

Regrettably, high challenged, deeply committed keys leaders look for pastors who look like them. They create a wider motivational gap. In this situation, I gently suggest to the key leaders and the pastor, "Good friends, your *challenge* is to develop a strong *commitment* to doing what you do out of the two motivational resources of *compassion* and *community*." This is the *reasonable* thing you can do…. focus on the motivational resources of compassion and community. This is where the grassroots live." This is a motivational *bridge*.

I will ask key leaders whether they have grandchildren. They do. They have pictures. They joyfully share their delight. They speak of all the good fun things they do with their grandchildren. They say, "If we knew how much fun grandchildren were going to be, we would have had them first."

I suggest to them that they, in fact, live the motivations of compassion and community with their grandchildren. These are the motivations present in their grandchildren. I suggest they will do well when they relate to the grassroots the same way they relate to their grandchildren. It is a motivational *bridge*.

Motivating Grass Roots

It happens again and again in congregations. People say to me, "Dr. Callahan, there are only a few of us who do everything." This happens because of a motivational gap. Often, the faithful few are motivated by commitment. Thus, the leadership recruitment is pitched toward commitment. The grass roots members do not respond to commitment. They respond best to compassion or community.

In thinking through how to raise funds for a fellowship hall and church school facilities, you can design a giving campaign to appeal to the persons who hope will be generous givers. Do you want to raise the money primarily with the key leaders? Do you want to raise the money primarily with the grass roots?

I once asked each person on the finance committee to list these six motivational resources on a sheet of paper. I invited each of them to think which two motivational resources influence the grass roots of their congregation.

I reminded them not to think about leaders but rather the grass roots. Independently and individually, each person of the finance committee checked "compassion and community" as the major motivational resources influencing the grass roots.

I said to them, "The best thing you can do is to launch the giving campaign with the best good-fun, good-times fellowship, community-oriented, family reunion supper this congregation has ever seen. In the brochure, do not focus on the square footage of the buildings. Instead, you can show *people pictures* of who will benefit from the new facilities.

Describe the mission and programs that will take place in the new facilities. Share how the new facilities will help advance forward person's lives and destinies in compassionate, community ways. Share how people will discover the grace of God."

These key leaders tended to motivate themselves primarily by challenge and commitment. They wanted to raise the money primarily from the grass roots. They remembered their grandchildren. They remembered what I had suggested.

They decided *not* to launch the campaign with a Loyalty Sunday that appealed to commitment. They decided *not* to have a "challenge thermometer goal" of a specific dollar amount that *must* be reached in order to do this project. They decided not to remind people of their "commitment vows."

They had done all of these things in previous campaigns. They had usually "fallen short." The giving had come mostly from key leaders. Little came from the grassroots.

I had told the finance committee, "If you prefer to raise the money from among *only* the key leaders in this congregation, be sure to focus on the motivations of challenge and commitment. You will raise the money primarily from among the key leaders.

This is what you have taught me about your previous campaigns. The lesson to learn is to focus on the motivational resources prevalent among the grass roots if you hope to raise the money with the grass roots.

In weak and declining and dying congregations, I find many of the key leaders originally became part of the congregation out of the motivations of compassion and community. But, over the past twenty-five years, the few remaining key leaders have changed the focus of their motivations to challenge and commitment. To be sure, the only people left are those people who are committed to the challenge of trying to keep this congregation going so that it might minimally survive.

I find reasonability a major motivation in communities that have a high density of engineers, scientists, and data processing persons. In small college towns, with a high density of professors, reasonability will be a major motivation.

Sometimes, I discover a congregation that has been badly burned by several traumatic events in recent years. In this setting, the key leaders learn the motivation of reasonability. Understandably, people in this situation will hesitate—want to make sure a plan makes good sense—before they put their hand into the flame yet another time. The last few times they did, they got burned.

Now, I have never yet met a couple who got married out of the motivation of reasonability. If it made reasonable sense, most people would not be married. People get married out of compassion, community, and hope. Then, they rationalize why it made sense to get married earlier rather than later.

An overworked motivation is commitment. Someone says to me, "Dr. Callahan, what we need in our congregation is people with more commitment." My response is "Good friend, you have just taught me you are a long-time Christian. The early motivations that draw all of us to the Christian life are compassion, community, and hope. Then, over twenty or more years, some people grow forward the motivation of commitment."

I add, "If there were lots of long-time Christians out there, we would do well on commitment. What are out there are persons who are unchurched....who are on the verge of beginning their early years in a Christian life."

I go on to suggest, "You have taught me that a major motivation out of which you do what you do is commitment. But, good friend, many persons do what they do in the congregation out of compassion, community, hope, challenge, or reasonability. You are wanting people to motivate themselves the way you motivate yourself. You will do better when you focus on the actual way people motivate themselves."

Some key leaders and pastors, with a primary motivation of commitment, press the congregation to "remember their membership vows." For persons for whom *compassion* is their primary motivation, the phrase "remember your membership vows" may end up sounding like "remember to clean up your room."

To be sure, the membership vows of many denominations were written by people whose primary motivation was commitment. They were long-time Christians when they wrote the vows.

The early vows are more like,

> "Will you love the Lord your God with all your heart, and mind, and soul, and strength?
> Will you love your neighbor as you love yourself?"

In some congregations, it would be helpful during giving campaigns to have compassion cards rather than commitment cards. It would make better sense to have a Love Sunday rather than a Loyalty Sunday. It would be more helpful to have a Community Sunday rather than a Commitment Sunday.

Motivations with Given Cultures

Given cultural groupings tend to have given motivations that are predominate in that culture. For a long time, the United States was a church culture. Many people went to church and church was a major force in the culture. It was the thing to do to go to church.

In a churched culture, commitment, reasonability, and challenge tended to be the major, dominate motivational resources.

Mostly, among the three, the two that were predominate were commitment and challenge.

We are, mostly, no longer a churched culture. We are more of what I would call a mission culture. We resonate more strongly with the motivations of compassion, community, and hope. And, mostly among the three, the two that are major are compassion and community.

We are coming to a millennial culture. Yes, we have an emerging millennial generation of eighty million persons. I mean more that that. With the eighty million millennial persons, we have a nearly overwhelming force of persons and groupings that are changing the nature of the whole culture.

In a millennial culture, the three primary motivations are hope, reasonability, and compassion. Hope comes first as a major motivation, primarily, for millennials, because there is no hope.

Millennials have done most everything they have been asked to do. They have done grade school, middle school, high school, university, and graduate school. And, they are still living in the bedroom of their parents' home, the bedroom into which they moved when they were three years old.

There is no hope.

They are told that their future will be less than their parents' future. The question of a house or, even, a car of consequence is open and uncertain. The jobs available do not look promising.

Hence, the longing for hope.

Hence, the equal longing for reasonability.

Mostly, millennials are good natured persons. They do not feel strongly betrayed. There is some sense of betrayal. Betrayal is here. They did think life was going to turn out somewhat better than it has. It has not.

Thus, they simply seek a future, a hope, that has some stability and reliability to it. They want not pie in the sky. They want no wishful thinking. They long for a hope that has a spirit of reasonability about it.

And, they have a deep motivation of compassion. This was not as true sometime back as it is now. They have found their way to this compelling motivation. There is a genuine longing for compassion. They have a yearning that their lives might count in some constructive way.

A possibility for growing the gift of hope is to actively build on the motivations with which God blesses you. Feel free to claim your primary motivations. Build on your major motivations. When we focus on a lesser motivation, we live in despair. Build on your key motivations. Do better what you do best.

Living in hope is building on your primary motivations.
Build on your primary motivations. Live in hope.
Living in hope is growing your major motivations.

Generosity

GOD BLESSES US WITH GENEROSITY.

God blesses you with your generosity. Live your generosity. You will live in hope. When we live with a conserving, holding, protecting, preserving spirit, we live in fear and misery. We do not live in hope.

"Tom is generous." "It is amazing all the people Tom helps." "Tom is among the most generous people I know." "Tom assists more people than anyone I have ever known." "When people think of Tom, they think of his generosity." "Tom is a legend for his amazing generosity."

Tom grew up poor. His father kicked him and his brother out of the home when they were still in elementary school. He did not want them any more. They were too much trouble. They were not wanted. He did not want to fool with them any more.

They were young, and now on their own.

They had a tough time. They fared for themselves for a while, doing this or that odd job. Sleeping in barns and doing chores here and there. Finally, they found steady work on a farm. Mostly, they put themselves through grade school. It was anything but easy.

High school ensued. College followed. Graduate school followed beyond that. There were, to be sure, scholarships and loans.

It was mostly working multiple jobs, part-time and full-time, long hours, hard work; studying late at night and on into the early morning. There was not a lot of time for much else.

There was laughter. There were good times. There were close friendships and new family. There were discoveries and insights. There was no resentment, no bitterness. There was no lamenting, complaining, whining, bemoaning. There was no bad-mouthing: woe is me, poor little me. There was graciousness and kindness.

It was more than making the best of a bad deal in life. It was moving on. Building one's life, as best one could, given the limited resources at hand. Tom's gift for understanding, loving, accepting, being generous with those who were down and out came from his having been there. He knew what it was like.

He never seemed to have much money. What he had, he gave away. It was not, I think, that he was a soft touch. It was more as if he had a deep compassion and a strong spirit of generosity. He would help in whatever ways he could. He gave his time. He provided food. He helped with some money. He provided a bed for the night and a bus ticket home.

He loved people. The lives he touched, the people he helped, the families who were restored, the youths who were inspired, their number is legion.

He wore himself out helping people.

He married. He and his wife had two children. He had countless friends. He lived a wondrous life. He is among the most generous persons I have ever known.

One key, one possibility, for a whole, healthy life is generosity. God invites us to a life of generosity, not grabbing and hoarding, conserving and holding, protecting and preserving.

Sharing the grace of generosity is one of the rare gifts in life. We are at our best when, amidst the scarcity and plenty, the shortness and the fullness, all of which abound, we discover the sources for a life of generosity and giving.

Tom had the sense that he was advancing and building his life effectively. He had the sense of being surrounded by the love of God. He had the confidence that his life counted, was worthwhile and constructive. He had a sense of where he was headed in life. He knew he was part of a winning cause. He shared his generosity in many ways.

Gracious receivers are generous givers.

As we graciously receive the grace and hope of God, we have the confidence that we can be generous givers. Reassurance comes from God. When we try to reassure ourselves, we take it upon ourselves to deal with our fear by ourselves. Our fear gets the best of us. We try harder to deal with our fear. We develop a fear of our fear. We try harder yet.

We receive the grace and hope of God. God's love pours forth to us, tumbling, rushing, spilling over like rivers in the wilderness. With the extraordinary love of God, we are at peace about our fear. We receive the calming, restoring spirit of God. We receive the healing, renewing grace of God.

We receive God's generosity. We become generous givers.

We live lives of modest financial needs. We value ourselves in more ways than money. We develop our financial resources. We share our blessings with many persons and causes.

Your generosity is a source of Hope Live your generosity. You will live in hope.

A possibility for coming to understand the gift of hope with which God blesses you is to live a life of generosity. Persons who share a spirit of generosity live a life of hope. Some persons are stingy and selfish, and they live lives of bitterness and resentment, dejection and despair.

Feel free to claim and share your generosity.

Build on your kindness and your bigheartedness. Yes, we do not contribute to dependence and co-dependence. We are wiser and more thoughtful than that. Our generosity is thoughtful and helpful.

Our generosity shares almost enough help to be helpful, and not so much help that the help becomes harmful and creates a pattern of dependency and co-dependency. We share a generosity that is helpful.

Tom had that remarkable ability. He knew how to share his spirit of generosity without creating co-dependency. He had a sense for knowing when his generosity was just right, not too little, and, more importantly, not too much.

The puzzle with generosity is sharing too much. Yes, some people make the mistake of sharing too little generosity. Most people make the terrible mistake of sharing too much generosity. In their desire to be of help, they go overboard. They want to help, and they give too much help.

The art is to share your generosity with balance, not excess.

Living in hope is living life with generosity.

God blesses you with God's Generosity:

one, because God is generous;
two, because God wants us to live lives of Generosity;
three, because we will then live in Hope.

Generosity and Hope are good friends.

When we live in Generosity, we live in Hope.

Passion

GOD BLESSES US WITH PASSION.

God blesses you with the gift of passion, with the gift of your passion. Live your passion. You will live in hope. Your passion is a source of Hope.

These days, I say to millennials, "Success is service." "Success is not salary." In an earlier time, the time of the baby boomers, it was appropriate to say, "Success is salary." More fully, "Success is salary, house, cars, vacations, comforts, and stuff." It was a time of hard work, steady positions, and comfortable lives.

No more.

In this time, we will want to discover a deeper understanding of success. These days, I suggest that success has to do more with passion and service than position and salary. More fully, I suggest, "Success is your passion. Live your passion. You will live in Hope.

Play your passion. Your passion is God's gift. Play to win. Play to serve. You will live in hope.

How you play the game teaches you whether you live in hope.

I was watching the Final Four in college basketball. That particular year, exciting, compelling basketball was being played in the final stages of the National College Basketball Tournament.

Toward half-time of one game, with a fast break and a full-court press, a team got ahead by twenty-plus points. They were acting on their game plan. They played an extraordinary first half. Their teamwork, speed, passing, shooting, and ability were amazing to behold. They played their passion.

They came out after half-time, and in the third quarter they began to lose their lead and fall disastrously behind. It was as if they were some other team.

The announcer of the game asked the coach-announcer what had happened. The coach-announcer said, "I've always taught my teams that we play to win. In the first and second quarters of the game, with their fast break and full-court press, this team played to win. They played their passion.

In the third quarter, they came out and began to play to avoid losing, and they got off their game, and that is why they fell behind."

I thought about that game for a long time.

I know people who *act*, who move forward, who live life with confidence and assurance: "I play to win." Their spirit is: "I count on accomplishing something worthwhile with my life."

They live not with a self-centered sense of self-promotion and self-aggrandizement, but with a spirit that says, "I want my life to count, in enduring, lasting ways. I count on making some constructive difference for the betterment of my family, my friends, for the advancement of humankind. I am growing my life now. I am living my passion"

I know some people whose life, regrettably, seems to say, "I play to avoid losing." There is no growth forward. They take a kind of retrenchment or retreat approach to life, and there is a sense of underlying despair. They may even be "ahead in the game, twenty-plus points." But they have developed a cautious, holding, trying-to-avoid-losing stance. They are off their game.

I know people whose approach to life is, "I play to lose." For various reasons they have developed an identity of failure. There is no action, no growth forward, and no passion.

Just about the time they get near success, they marshal all their considerable resources and competencies to ensure they fail once again. For them to succeed would create an identity crisis. It would challenge their notion that they always fail. So they ensure that they lose yet again.

I know people whose approach to life is, "I am not certain I plan to leave the locker room. It is safer and more secure here." But there is little life and no action in a locker room.

The game is won on the field, not in the locker room. The locker room is not where life is lived out. Some preparation can take place in a locker room, but the game itself is played on the field.

The truth is, all of us sometimes—at various stages of life, even on various days of the week – live life all these ways:

I play to win.
I play to avoid losing.
I play to lose.
I am not certain I plan to leave the locker room.

We find ourselves, from time to time, involved with each.

When we live "I play to win," we help those around us. Innately, we know we are created by God to live life this way, to live the passion with which God blesses us.

We are drawn to people who live with this integrity and spirit. When we live life any of the other three ways, routinely, dully, we do not help ourselves, and we do not help those around us. They already have difficulty with those other three ways in their own lives.

Misery may love company, but people are smart enough to know they do not need the mixed blessing of a person who is in no better shape than they are, and who is not advancing his or her life. When we act on our life, when we grow our life, when we live our passion, we help other persons act on and grow their life, live their passion.

Focus

Your gift of passion tends to have a specific focus. The possibilities are virtually endless. For some, the focus of their passion may be:

Athletic
Intellectual
Extracurricular
Social
Music
Arts
Computer
Games
Cooking
Quilting
Building
Traveling
Work
Projects
Fad
Outcast
Entrepreneurial
The list of passions goes on and on.

For Lorie, her passion is quilting. She has, to date, created more than eighty quilts. Her stash of fabrics suggests many more quilts are on the horizon. For Bob, his passion is Chess. He is a Master. He loves to play. It is his passion.

For Jim, his passion is bridge. Local and state tournaments abound. His memory of the bridge tournaments in which he has competed is phenomenal. For Anne and Paul, their passion is sailing. The breezes stir their passion, and they are off to distant horizons. For Gene and Ann, their passion is cooking. They love to gather friends and share a meal.

For many persons, their vocation is their passion. They love what they do. Their identity is in their work. Their work is who they are. For many persons, their friendships are their passion. They are who they are by the friendships they create and share. Their passion is not in achievements and accomplishments. Their passion is in the roots, place, and belonging of the family and friendships they share across the span of their lives.

Variety

Your gift of passion may vary from time to time across the course of your life. Yes, for some persons, their passion is consistently the same passion for their lifetime.

They fall in love with one passion, and, for them, this is the fullness and wholeness of their one wonderful, remarkable passion as their years go by.

For many, many persons, they move from one passion to another as their years come and go. Their passion, for a time, may be a given sport. Then, they may grow forward a passion for a given vocation. Then, later on, they may develop a passion for given charitable cause. Still later, they may share a passion with a given hobby – a model railroading club.

The variety of passions a person develops has something to do with the creativity they seek to live out in the course of their life. It is not because they are easily bored. They have many interests and they enjoy exploring them with considerable passion.

For many persons in the Mt. Princeton area where I have written the majority of my books, their passion has a seasonal focus. In the summer, their passion is rafting the Arkansas River or hiking in the mountains. As the snows of winter come, their passion becomes skiing down the snow covered slopes. There are seasonal passions.

Intensity

Passion comes in varied intensities. Your passion may be experienced as a deep yearning and an intense longing. Your passion may be experienced as a quiet desire and a gentle craving. It is not the case that passion only occurs in an intense, throbbing spirit. We experience passion across a spectrum of intensity.

---

quiet desire	deep yearning
gentle craving	intense longing

A given event of passion may range from one end of the spectrum to the other. Likewise, another event of passion may be consistently at one point of the spectrum, and never vary across the spectrum.

You will have fun assessing which events of passion demonstrate where they tend to show up on the spectrum of intensity and under what circumstances. You will better understand yourself as you discover the patterns of intensity with which you live your life.

Duration

Likewise, you will have fun discovering the duration, the length of time, a given event of passion tends to endure. Passion may endure with deep intensity for the whole of one's life. Passion may endure for a period of time, be at rest for a time, and return with renewed vigor for an intense period of time.

The art is to encourage your passion to have a natural duration. Do not force the gift of your passion. Your passion will flow at its natural depth when you allow the nature of the gift to be free and creative.

When you share the gift of your passion with a spirit of grace and gratitude, your passion will be at its natural best. When you try to force it forward, it becomes stilted and awkward, clumsy and artificial.

Number

For many, many persons, one compelling passion is sufficient for one life time. We can think of countless persons who have lived their whole lives with one passion. They are blessed of God.

And, there is no necessary merit in living only one passion. Many, many persons live, for a time, one extraordinary passion; then, they discover a second helpful passion. They discover an equal spirit of grace and satisfaction with their second passion.

Many, many persons discover two complementary passions and live both passions forward in mutually helpful ways. Yes, you already sense where I am heading.

People have the energy to live forward two, perhaps three, even four passions at one time.

Passion stirs energy. Energy sustains passion. And, it stretches both passion and energy to try to sustain five, six, or seven distinctive passions. We are wiser to focus on one, two, or three passions at a time. When we stretch our passions too thin, we diminish the power of our passion. When we diminish the power of our passion, we diminish our spirit of hope.

A possibility for growing the gift of hope with which God blesses you is to live a life of passion. Persons who live a life of passion live a life of hope. Some persons lack passion; they lack hope.

Feel free to live your passion. Build on your intensity and force. Be not shy and bashful, timid and reticent. By the same token, one need not be noisy and loud. Persons with passion can be quietly forceful.

Passion is a wondrous gift of God that stirs our best selves to move forward.

God gives us the gift of passion so we can live in hope.

Memories

GOD BLESSES US WITH OUR MEMORIES.

God blesses you with your memories. Gather your Memories. You will live in hope. Your memories are a source of Hope. You will live in hope.

God blesses you with:
    your memories
    your present
    your immediate future
    your distant future
    your next life future, beyond the River

Some persons talk about two selves: the present self and the future self. They seek to differentiate between the present self and the future self, that we live both in the present and we live in the future.

My wisdom is that there are five possibilities for our self:
1. Our past self is with us in our memories.
2. Our present self is with us in our present life.
3. Our future self is with us in our immediate future.
4. Our future self is with us in our distant future.
5. Our future self is with us in our next life future.

We live in the midst of these five possibilities that give richness and texture to our lives.

> I confirm this,
> Hope is stronger than memory.
> Memory is strong.
> Hope is stronger.

We live on hope more than memory. Take away a person's memories and we become anxious. Take away a person's hopes and we become terrified.

> I confirm this,
> Memory is strong.

Memory is strong because memory is about **_incidental events_**. We do not know quite why we remember them. And, they are there, in our memory. Simple things. A home in which we lived. A day at school. A nick nack we picked up somewhere. A meal we had. Some old clothes we once wore, and remember with fondness.

We remember the building of a snowman in the cold winter of northern Ohio, with its wet from Lake Erie full, moist snow. It would hold together well, for snowmen, forts, and snow balls.

We remember the coming of spring, with the singing of the birds, the budding of the trees, and the promise of warmer weather.

We remember a gathering at the town's swimming pool in the summer's heat. A game of monopoly we enjoyed, laughing and carrying on, late into the night. A walking to the corner, neighborhood grocery store for a candy bar or ice cream cone. An ordinary day of summer. Nothing special. We somehow remember.

Memory is strong because memory is about **_tragic events_** that mar and scar our lives. A car accident, with a light changing and one car in a hurry to cross the intersection. Two are injured. Two are dead. An unexpected disaster, with the coal mine filling with smoke and heat and fire. A quick illness and sudden death, with youth at stake, and finally the losing of life.

A relationship gone awry, with bitterness and resentment, despair and depression creating and widening a huge gulf between once good friends. A twisted and turning of good intentions that ended in unplanned misfortune, with the slacking of hope and future. The swift coming of a tidal wave that wipes out whole villages and towns and thousands of people, who were simply enjoying the pleasantry of a beautiful summer day at the beach.

Memory is strong because memory is about **_sinful events_** for which we ask the forgiveness of God and the forgiveness of others, mostly loved ones, we have wronged. We look back and see the tattered trail of sinful events in which we have participated. Most of them were not intentional. Some were. We regret.

Mostly, we did not intend to participate in these sinful events. Somehow, we did. They are grevious to us. We wish we could undo them. For some events, we have made amends. For some, we have not done so. For some, we know it would be harmful, at this point, to seek to make amends.

These sinful events are with us. We remember these events. Their power over us is immense. We wish we could let go of their painful memories. We are sad. We weep. We long for the forgiveness that is like a spring rain that washes the pollen from the air and the grasses and brings a new smell to the air and a new spirit to the land.

Memory is strong because memory is about **_celebrative events_**. Birthdays. Proms. Dances, especially first dances. Close, winning games, with our home team scoring in the final seconds.

A First Date, with the promise of the days and years to come. Going steady, with the discovery of the deeper love for one another. Engagement, for which we are grateful to God.

Wedding, with the promise of the years to come. Children, with many people congratulating us and blessing the new born child. Anniversaries. Graduations. New positions. Promotions. Recognitions. Reunions, with the gathering of classmates, family, and close friends. Special occasions. Now here, now there, gatherings of family and friends. We remember these special times. They are strong in our lives.

These good times help us beyond the tragic times and the sinful times that so weigh us down. We enjoy the celebrations of life, family, and friends.

Most of all, memory is strong because memory is about **_hope fulfilled events_**. These events are the events in which our deepest longings and richest yearnings are fulfilled. We remember them because they are the events of hope that have been fulfilled. The Passover. The Exodus. The Manger. The Teachings. The Open Tomb. The Risen Lord. The Resurrection.

These events give us confidence and assurance for the present and the future that is now before us. These telling events show us that the promise of the future has been fulfilled and is being fulfilled.

When we cannot find hope in the present, we postpone our hopes to the immediate future. When we cannot find hope in the immediate future, we postpone our hopes to the distant future.

When we cannot find hope in the present, the immediate future, and the distant future, we postpone our hopes to the next life future, beyond the river, to the time to come in the life to come.

We long for hope. We yearn for hope. We search for hope.

In our search for hope, we are sometimes the Flimsies People. Sometimes, we are the Cliff People. Sometimes, we are the River People. Sometimes, we are the Easter People.

Sometimes, we are **_the Flimsies People_**. We see no hope.

We see no hope in the immediate future, the distant future, or the next life future beyond the river. We long for hope. We see no hope. We yearn for hope. We see no hope.

So we grasp for the fleeting flimsies of this life, the new outfit, the new car, the new job, the new house, the new trinket, the new gadget, the new game, the new toy.

We search for the kinds of flimsies hopes the world offers.

We look for the false hopes the world promises. We settle for the world's understanding of hope. We cave into the world's sham, fragile, feeble notions of hope.

We look for sources of hope among the flimsies of this life.

Even as we do, we know that they are shadows of hope. They do not last.

Sometimes, we are **_the Cliff People_**. We are frozen on the face of a cliff.

Think what it is like to find oneself on the face of a cliff. The wind is blowing. The weather is getting colder. We can see no handholds and footholds ahead. We can see no way back to the handholds and footholds behind.

What do we do in that predicament?

We do one thing extraordinarily well. We freeze to the face of the cliff, clinging and clutching for dear life, fixed and immobile. We want no change. There is a very excellent reason we want no change! Because the only change we can see is the gulf, the chasm, the abyss below.

For some, inaction, doing nothing, is the fear of making a mistake. The best way to never make a mistake, to run aground on a coral reef, is to never leave the dock, to do nothing.

For many persons, inaction, doing nothing, is the fear of plummeting to the abyss below. For many, they can see no handholds and footholds ahead, and they have lost the ability to reach back to the handholds and footholds behind.

They freeze.

We are wrestling with inaction not due to apathy, laziness, indifference, not caring. Oh, a few may do nothing for those reasons.

Being hard on people, whipping people, assuming the task is to motivate them from inaction to action does not work. Their inaction is not due to lethargy and indifference.

We wrestle with a deeper dilemma, a far more pervasive and profound difficulty. Many, many people do nothing because they are frozen on the face of a cliff. They see no hope. They become immobile. They freeze.

The person frozen to the face of the cliff is disrupted, alarmed, frightened even more. The person either clutches more fiercely frozen, determined not to move. Or, worse, the person, rattled and upset, loses the handholds and footholds they have so carefully held onto, and falls into the chasm and abyss below.

What one does is join the person on the face of the cliff and gently and quietly coach them forward. Let's try the left hand. Three inches up. Here is this handhold. Now, the left foot. Two inches. Here is this foothold. Now, here is another handhold. Now, here is this foothold. Gently, quietly, inch by inch, we coach the person forward to new handholds and footholds.

When we find ourselves nearly frozen on the face of a cliff, we gently and quietly coach ourselves forward. We discover some person or group who helps us to new handholds and new footholds, to new sources of hope.

Sometimes, we cling to this brief frailty we call life; we cling and clutch so hard that we miss the thrill and joy of simply being alive. We are so concerned about losing life, that we never really find it. We stay frozen to the cliff.

Sometimes, we are **_the River People_**. We postpone our hopes to the next life beyond the River.

At New Liberty Church, when the kids rode their horses across the church cemetery, people got upset, not simply because they thought the horses and the kids were desecrating the ancestors of the past. To be sure, there was that.

More so, people were upset because the horses and the kids were trampling on the church's symbol of the future. That church cemetery is not primarily a symbol of the past. The people know that those who are buried there are not really there.

They want to be buried there, not so they can lie beside so and so, and share in late night conversations. Though, when I walk by late some nights, I sometimes hear the mutterings and the murmurings.

People want to be buried there because the cemetery is the symbol of each family's entrance into the kingdom of hope beyond this life. To be sure, the cemetery honors those who have gone before.

Most important, the focus is on where they have gone. They have gone to a new and promised land, to the land of hope. People want to be buried there, importantly because that cemetery is equally and fully their symbol of the future. They only fix the cemetery up one a year, just before homecoming.

Many, many churches across our country have a homecoming each year. These are not events that look to the past only. Church homecomings are events that look to the future. The homecoming is a present day, looking forward, foretelling, proleptic event that looks to that "great homecoming beyond the river" when we will all be gathered as God's family.

Some make the mistake of thinking their task is to drag people reluctantly from the customs, habits, and traditions of the past into the present. They work hard to get people to give up their past. They miss the fact that many people are not living in the past.

They are living in the next-life future. Many have postponed their hopes to the next life. They can see no way in which even some of their hopes will be fulfilled in the present, immediate, or even distant future. So, they are living in the next-life future.

The art is to help them discover the realization of some of their hopes in the distant future, the immediate future, and the present. Hope happens now. The art is not to drag them from a distant past.

The art is to help them discover concrete sources of hope now. They do not need to postpone their hopes to the next life beyond the River.

Sometimes we are the river people. We postpone our hope to the next life beyond the river.

When we live life at our best, we are ***the Easter People***. We live with confidence and assurance that we are the People of Hope. We live with the spirit and encouragement that we are the people of the open tomb, the Risen Lord, and new life in Christ. We live in Hope.

A possibility for valuing the gift of hope with which God blesses you is to remember your memories. Persons who remember their memories live a life of hope. The richness of your memories gives confidence and assurance to your hopes. Some persons lack the fullness of their memories; they lack hope.

Feel free to resonant with your memories. Your memories are a source of hope. One need not dwell on them. By the same token, one need not forget them. Your memories are a wondrous gift of God that stirs our best selves to move forward.

God blesses you with your memories. Gather your Memories. You will live in hope. Your memories will stir your hopes.

God blesses us with the gift of our memories so we can live with hope.

Mentors

GOD BLESSES US WITH OUR MENTORS.

God blesses you with your Mentors. Your mentors are a source of Hope. Gather your Mentors. You will live in hope.

> Therefore, seeing we also are surrounded
> about with so great a cloud of witnesses,
> let us lay aside every weight and sin
> that so weights us down,
> and let us run with perseverance
> the race that is set before us.
> Hebrews 12:1

Each morning, when you wake up, gather your mentors. Live this day in the presence of your mentors. You will live this day in hope. Across the years, I have shared this insight with countless persons across the planet. Again and again, people teach me how helpful this daily practice is with them.

God comes to us directly, with grace. Christ comes to us directly, with peace. The Spirit comes to us directly, with hope. And, God sends us our mentors so we will live in grace, peace, and hope. Our mentors are our mentors, precisely because they bring us clues, possibilities, sources of hope.

I came to this discovery in this way.

I was helping a congregation and a pastor. It is a solid congregation and a solid pastor. John is a good shepherd, a wise, caring leader, and a community pastor.

On a Sunday morning, I watched as John slowly, carefully, precisely, and meticulously read a twenty plus long, long manuscript sermon without ever looking up once during the twenty plus long, long minutes.

After the service, with a spirit of expectancy and hopefulness, John asked me what I thought of the sermon.

Now, I have had the honor of helping many, many pastors and congregations across many years. I am wise. I am wise enough to know that I do not discuss a sermon with a pastor on Sunday.

I do not even discuss the sermon with the pastor on Monday. Some pastors are tired. With some pastors, there is still just enough despair and depression left over from Sunday. "Why did I say this? I could have said this. The second guesses, the recriminations, the possibilities are still there on Monday."

I dearly love A & W root beer. I had spotted one of the old A & W root beer stands in the community. It had booths, tables, and a counter inside. I said to John, "Tuesday morning, at our break, ten- ten thirty, I will treat us to an A & W root beer and we will have fun visiting about the sermon. It will be my treat."

On Tuesday morning, at our break, we headed to the A & W root beer stand. We got the two tall, large, ice cold, frosted mugs. The A & W root beer is good out of the bottle or the can. It is really good out of the faucet, in an ice cold mug.

We found a corner booth. We enjoyed our first sips of the ice cold root beer. Then, John said to me, eagerly and expectantly, "Now, Dr. Callahan share with me what you thought of the sermon I preached on Sunday."

Picking up a sheet of paper, holding it in front of me as though I were reading from it, I said in a gentle, easygoing way, "John, teach me where you learned to read, slowly, carefully, precisely, meticulously, a twenty plus long, long, long manuscript sermon without ever looking up once during the whole twenty plus long, long, long minutes."

"You did not learn that in seminary. Even there, in seminary, we teach you to look up three times – once for each of the three points in the sermon. I call this the Trinitarian Look-up."

We thought and thought. We puzzled and puzzled. We considered this and that.

The clue came, finally, when John described how, during the spring semester of his senior year in seminary, he and his fiancée were married. Graduating from seminary, they went eagerly and expectantly, with much excitement, to serve their first congregation.

Their new church was just near enough to her parents that each Sunday for the three years they served their first congregation, that her parents came, proud, beaming, and smiling, to worship in their daughter and son-in-law's church.

And, it was just near enough to his in-laws home, that each Sunday after worship, he and his new bride would go to her parents' home for a wonderful Sunday meal.

As they would be sitting down to a bountiful meal, his new father-in-law, beaming and proud, well-intentioned and well-meaning, would pull from his inside coat pocket, the little black note book of corrections he had made while listening to his new son-in-law's sermon that morning.

Syntax. Sentence structure. Synonyms. Learned, impressive words. These many corrections would improve the sermon. For three long, long, long years, each Sunday after worship, this well-meaning, correcting session had taken place.

John was a competent pastor. Nevertheless, those correcting session, as well-meaning as they were intended to be, had created a pastor who, in the years come and gone, would read, slowly, carefully, precisely, meticulously, a twenty plus long, long, long manuscript sermon without ever looking up once during the whole twenty plus long, long, long minutes.

So that he would be sure to never make a mistake again!

I found an A & W paper napkin. Lots of good things are drawn on A & W paper napkins. I drew a diagram of the worship space of his church, the pews, the pulpit, the choir loft, etc. I then said to John, "Show me where your father-in-law is sitting each Sunday morning as you read your manuscript sermon."

John said, "Oh, no, my father-in-law died ten years ago."

I picked up the same sheet of paper I had used earlier to signify his manuscript sermon. I held it in front of me, as I had done before, as though reading from it.

Without looking up, slowly, carefully, precisely, meticulously, I said, "Well, he may have died ten years ago, but he is still showing up every Sunday. On the diagram of your church, show me where he is sitting."

And he knew!

John knew right where his father-in-law had sat every Sunday during those early three long, long, long years making careful, meticulous notes in his cherished little black note book. He sat on the outside end of the second pew, at the front, on the left side from the pastor's view. We marked his place on our diagram of John's church.

I encouraged John, "Think of a mentor who has meant much to you during your life's pilgrimage. An encourager, a coach, a nurturer. Someone who has drawn forth the best in you. Someone who has helped you live your life at your best. Someone who has helped you to grow forward. Teach me who comes to mind."

"Dorothy," he said.

Dorothy was from a previous church. She had been a mentor and coach with John. She was an encourager and nurturer.

I said, "This coming Sunday, as you look out before you begin the Service, and before you begin the Sermon, where will Dorothy be sitting?"

"Oh, no, Dorothy lives clear across the state. It would be too far. She couldn't make it on time," John said.

Picking up the same sheet of paper I had used earlier to signify his manuscript sermon, I held it in front of me, as I had done before, as though reading from it.

Without looking up, slowly, carefully, precisely, meticulously, I said,

> "Yes, and your father-in-law lives clear across the
> River on the other side in the next life with God."
> He is still showing up each Sunday. If he can make
> it from that far away and show up, so can Dorothy.
> It is a shorter trip."

He knew immediately where she would be sitting, where in a previous church, her presence, encouragement, coaching, and mentoring, had meant much to him.

> "Right there. Half way back in the center of the pew
> on the left side of the sanctuary from my view from
> the pulpit."

We marked where Dorothy would be sitting this coming Sunday.

I said to John, "Teach me a second mentor who comes to mind. Show me where he or she will be sitting this coming Sunday."

"Jim," he said. And John knew right where Jim would be sitting. Toward the front, third row back, on the right hand side from the pulpit.

Now, teach me a third mentor who has helped you to grow, whose presence and encouragement has meant much to you."

"Sue." Without my asking, he knew immediately where Sue would be sitting this coming Sunday. John noted,

> "She always slipped in just as the service began, sat on the outside aisle on the back row, and slipped out just as the service was ending."

I then said to John,

> "This coming Sunday and every Sunday hereafter, before the service begins, and especially before you stand to begin your sermon, I want you to look out and see Dorothy, and Jim, and Sue. Give me half a chance; I'll be sitting there too, right beside Dorothy."

A sense of peace came into his being. His face relaxed. His tenseness began to disappear. His anxiety lessened. He seemed more himself.

We were having so much fun, discovering new ways forward; we decided to treat ourselves to a second, ice cold A & W root beer.

As we were sitting down again, I said, "John, share with me something your father-in-law enjoyed doing in life."

"Traveling. He loved to travel," John said.

"Well," I said, "this coming Sunday let him travel. He has probably never been to the Himalayas. He will send a postcard back, 'Having a great time. The mountains are really high. Remember your synonyms.'"

"The next Sunday you could let him travel to Manchuria. Not many people ever get to Manchuria. The next Sunday you could let him travel to Mongolia. I hear it's pretty this time of year. The next Sunday he could enjoy the Antarctica. The penguins will welcome him gladly."

John took the pencil he had been using to mark his mentors on the chart. He drew an arrow from where his father-in-law's seat had been marked. The arrow went beyond the church wall to the outside to symbolize he was letting his father-in-law travel.

John and I had a grand visit. The gatherings with his congregation were warm and enthusiastic, thoughtful and helpful.

Some time passed.

I received a letter from John. He thanked me for the long-range plan we had developed together with his congregation. He thanked me for the A & W root beers we had shared together. He especially wanted to thank me for the A & W paper napkin.

You see, he had asked me to let him keep it, and our drawings on it.

He told me in his letter that the A & W napkin sits on his pulpit. Each Sunday, as he begins the service and the sermon, John looks out and sees his mentors, Dorothy, Jim, Sue, and Ken. They are with him. He has a sense of their presence. He has the assurance of the hope of God. He has the confidence of his message of the morning.

John went on to share with me, "Dr. Callahan, we are all grateful to you. We are experiencing the moving, stirring, living presence of the grace of God in ways we have not previously known. We are more at peace. We are more hopeful for our future, both for our lives and for our congregation. Thank you. God bless you."

God blesses us with our mentors so that we can live in hope.

Dr. Joseph Politella is among my mentors. I met Dr. Politella the first quarter of my Freshmen year at the university. I took his introductory course in Philosophy. I went on to take every course he taught. Philosophy became my Major.

He was a wise person. He was a remarkable teacher. He was of modest height and thin build. He spoke softly, with a gentle smile. He loved discovering new insights. He was kind and gentle. He was like an ancient wise man of old. We discovered the world with his help.

Dr. Politella and his wife, Sue, would have some of us as students, Majors in Philosophy, over to their home from time to time. These were special gatherings. The conversations were informal. We were invited to share discoveries. We were encouraged to ask questions. We learned much.

Think now, of the mentors with which God blesses you. Call them to mind. Picture them with you. See them sharing with you. Hear their voices. Sense their presence. Experience their compassion. Remember their wisdom. Let them bless you now. Live in hope.

Consider all of the times your mentors have encouraged you and coached you. Think of specific events where they have been decisively helpful to you.

A possibility in coming to understand the gift of hope with which God blesses you is to remember your mentors. Persons who remember their mentors live a life of hope. The encouragement of your mentors, the coaching with which they have helped you, the wisdom they have shared with you.... all these resources give you confidence and assurance, a deep, abiding spirit of hope.

Feel free to enjoy the blessings of your mentors. Your mentors are a source of hope. Your mentors are wondrous gifts of God that stirs our best selves to move forward. God blesses you with your Mentors. Your mentors are a source of Hope. Gather your Mentors. You will live in hope.

God blesses us with the gift of our mentors so we can live in hope.

Some Changes

GOD BLESSES US WITH SOME CHANGES.

God blesses you with some changes. Some changes are sources of hope. Encourage some changes. You will live in hope.

Throughout our lives we will experience change. Some change will be modest and small. Some changes will be major and huge. Since we are going to experience change, the art is to learn how to deal with change. We can learn the art of change.

When we learn to create some changes, albeit small, in our lives, we are able to participate in larger changes. When we help to shape some changes, we are better able to deal with more changes. When we do not help to shape some changes, we are less able to deal with change.

Practice change.

Practice simple changes.

When you have always put on the shoe for your right foot first, put on the shoe today for your left foot first. When you have always eaten your meat first, and then your potatoes; today eat your potatoes first.

When you have always started the car, and then put on your seat belt, today put on your seat belt first, and then start the car. When you have always started a walk by stepping out on your right foot first, today start your walk with your left foot first.

Practice simple, little changes from one day to the next. This practice helps us to be better able to deal with bigger changes. The person who "practices no changes, not ever" is in a tougher situation to deal with big changes when they come, let alone helping to create big changes.

God is the author of change….hope. Change is God's testimony of hope. Change is God's promise of hope. Security is not in stability. Security is in the wings, not the nest. The mother eagle pushes her babes from nest so they learn to fly. They do not learn to fly by staying in the nest.

Security is in change, not sameness. Grace stirs, not stays. God makes all things new. Rev. 21:5 We become who we are as we discover how to fly, how to grow forward some change in our lives.

Perfectionism discourages change. A compulsive addictive perfectionism discourages the developing and growing spirit of change. By definition, a compulsive addictive perfectionism wants things to stay the same.

Some where, along the way, in the course of life, we learn, we discover, we harbor a hidden, compulsive addictive perfectionism. Note the word, "discover." The word honors the thought that a compulsive addictive perfectionism tries to stay hidden. It prefers not to be noticed. It is like a virus not wanting to draw attention to itself. It seeks to do damage in the background, unnoticed, silent.

Some of us become perfectoholics. Perfectoholics.

Practice makes perfect. Yes, a natural, relaxed practice creates a natural, relaxed perfect. A compulsive, addictive practice creates a compulsive, addictive perfect.

Tense, tight practice creates tense, tight perfect. When we relax and have fun in the practice, we create a relaxed, having fun perfect.

Perfectionism is the world's notion of hope. We are not born with a compulsive addictive perfectionism. We learn this, usually from someone who "has our best interests at heart."

Yes, in music we want to be in tune, to hit the helpful note. Persons who do this well, do so with a natural ease and grace. Persons with an on-board compulsive addictive perfectionism, hit the right note, not with ease and flow, but striving, nervous, anxious to do so. They both hit the right note. One has fun. The other strives.

Two persons use the same golf club. They hit their ball the same distance. The one does it with grace and ease. The other does it, tense, tight, nervous, anxious – these are the four gifts of compulsive addictive perfectionism. The one enjoys the game. The other fights the game, all the way around the course.

When we discover our compulsive addictive perfectionism, we will discover our low self esteem. The two are good friends. When we find one, we find both. A compulsive addictive perfectionism has as its quiet message, "Sammy, you can do better." Translation: "Sammy, you never do good enough." Translation: "Sammy, you always fail."

Hope is stronger than perfectionism. Perfectionism leads to despair. Despair leads to hope.

Perfectionism and low esteem go together. The more we fail, the lower our self esteem. The lower our self esteem, the more compulsive our perfectionism.

Perfectionism, low self esteem, and wishful thinking go together. Gather your wishful thinking. You will gather your perfectionism, your low self esteem, and your wishful thinking. Wishful thinking leads to waiting on something to happen. Usually, the something to happen is outside ourselves, a saving of the situation by some outside force, a *Deus Ex Machina.*

Coupled with a wish to "never make a mistake" we stay at the dock. We do not set sail. In the Bahamas, the phrase is, "the skipper who says he has never run aground, his boat has never left the dock." Perfectionism, low self esteem, wishful thinking, wanting to never make a mistake, and waiting at the dock are a mixture for never doing anything, or always, or most always, always doing nothing..

We do not wrestle with apathy, laziness, and indifference. We wrestle with a hidden opponent that begins with compulsive addictive perfectionism that breeds low self esteem, that breeds wishful thinking, that breeds never make a mistake.

Inaction follows.

Despair follows.

When we discover our compulsive perfectionism, we discover our defeats, depression, and despair. Despair is really multiple despairs. Despair comes in threes and fours and fives and tens. Here a despair, there a despair. Now a despair, then a despair. Despair multiples. Despair grows faster and faster, deeper and deeper. Despair whirls like a merry-go-round, whirls and blurs, ever deepening our defeats, depressions, and despairs.

One can never, finally, achieve a compulsive addictive perfectionism. Perfectionism is always one more over the horizon.... Perfectionism is a never ending horizon of defeat and despair.... We can never achieve more.

Discover your perfectionism. Gather your low self esteem, your wishful thinking, your never make a mistake. Gather your inaction. Gather your despairs. In the midst of all these, you will discover hope.

Perfectionism, eventually, brings us to our knees. When we are on our knees, we discover hope. Hope is stronger than perfectionism. "Perfectionism" breeds "low self-esteem" breeds "wishful thinking" breeds "never make a mistake" breeds "staying at the dock" breeds "inaction" breeds "failure" breeds "defeat, depression, despair."

Hope is stronger than low self-esteem. Low self-esteem is the tendency to think more poorly of ourselves than we have a right to. High self-esteem is our over compensation for low self-esteem. We over compensate. We create a vicious cycle.

Then, with enormous generosity, we receive the grace of God, the peace of Christ, the hope of the Spirit.

Hope is stronger than failure and defeat. We have enough failures, excellent mistakes, in our own right without setting ourselves up with a compulsive, addictive perfectionism to insure we have more failures, mostly imaginary.

Hope is stronger than wishful thinking, a passive waiting for something to fall out of the sky, and save the day. Yes, wishful thinking is strong. Hope is stronger.

Hope is specific and concrete, active and moving forward. Hope builds on our strengths, not our weaknesses. Hope does not wait. Hope moves forward, marches. Hope never waits. Hope runs. Runs, leading us toward the future God is promising and preparing for us.

Perfectionism breeds despair. Despair brings us to hope. Hope is the gift of God in your life.

Hope is stronger than defeat, depression, despair. Yes, despair, depression, and defeat are good friends with each other. Grace, peace, hope are stronger good friends with one another.

We do not overcome our defeat, depression, and despair. We receive the grace of God. We discover peace with Christ. We are led by the hope of the Spirit. Thence, we live whole, healthy lives.

Hope is stronger than perfectionism
Perfectionism breeds failure.
Failure breeds despair.

Despair breeds low self-esteem.
Low self esteem breeds wishful thinking.
Wishful thinking breeds perfectionism.

Hope breaks the circle.

We live forward. We no longer live in a circle.

Hope is stronger than failure and defeat. We have enough failures, enough excellent mistakes in our own right without setting ourselves up with compulsive addictive perfectionism to insure we have yet more failures.

When we practice small changes in our daily lives, we are learning how to overcome a compulsive addictive perfectionism. A compulsive addictive perfectionism "needs" everything to stay the same. As we practice small changes, we free ourselves from the compulsive addictive perfectionism.

Hope is stronger than despair, depression, despondency, defeat. Yes, despair, depression, despondency, and defeat are good friends with each other. These four friends commiserate well with one another.

Hope is stronger than low self-esteem. Living in low self-esteem we think more poorly of ourselves than we have a right to. High self-esteem is our effort to over compensation for low self-esteem.

Hope is stronger than wishful thinking – a passive waiting for something to fall out of the sky, a something happening to save the day. Wishful thinking is strong. Hope is stronger.

Hope is specific and concrete. Hope is active, moving forward. Hope practices small changes. Hope builds on our strengths, not our weaknesses. Hope does not wait. Hope moves forward, marches. Hope never waits.

Some changes are helpful. Not all changes are helpful. Some changes are disasters. They do not encourage creativity, growth, and moving forward. They stultify, retard, and diminish the strengths, gifts, and competencies with which God blesses us.

Yes, not all changes are helpful. There is no value in change for the sake of change. There is no merit in advocating change for its own sake. There is no purpose in pressing change just to have change.

Some one once said, "Let's change." The other person said, "Yes, let's change. You go first." Such a conversation misses the point. There is no value in change for the sake of change.

Change is helpful when change advances grace and compassion, grows peace and calm, and stirs hope and encouragement. These changes advance the whole of humanity in constructive, helpful ways.

A possibility for growing the gift of hope with which God blesses you is to value some change. God blesses you with some change. Feel free to enjoy some change in your life. Practice some change. Give up a compulsive addictive perfectionism. This compulsive addictive perfectionism resists change....resists hope. Hope encourages change. Change encourages hope.

God blesses you with some changes. Some changes are sources of hope. Encourage some changes. You will live in hope.

God blesses us with the gift of change so we can live in hope.

Outcomes

GOD BLESSES US WITH OUTCOMES.

God blesses us with outcomes. Live on the outcomes. You will live in hope.

I begin this part of our conversation by reflecting on the variety and richness of the sermons I have been blessed to hear, in the years come and gone.

Across the years, I have heard many different sermons.

A shepherding sermon
A motivational sermon
A teaching sermon
A missional sermon
An outcome sermon

I have also heard many sermons of this nature

An elocutionary sermon
A muddled sermon
A quotational sermon
A fury and anger sermon
A barren desert sermon

A fluff and frizzy sermon
A managerial sermon
An institutional sermon
An apocalyptic sermon

A shepherding sermon has a pastoral, caring concern, touching the lives of persons. Such a sermon has the outcome of helping persons with some human hurt and hope in their lives.

A motivational sermon seeks to stir and inspire people to some action. The outcome of such a sermon is that some action happens, usually with a strong result.

A teaching sermon has an educational, instructional focus. The outcome is that people's understanding and knowledge is advanced and deepened.

An elocutionary sermon seeks to advance the message through the alliteration and poetry of the words.

A missional sermon seeks to grow forward some missional focus with unchurched persons. The outcome is that the Christian message is advanced with persons who are not yet part of the Christian movement.

Likewise, across the years, I have experienced a myriad of muddled and confused sermons. It is hard to know where these sermons are heading, if anywhere. They remind me of Alice in Alice and Wonderland, who asks of the Cheshire Cat, "Which road will I take?"

The Cheshire Cat responds with the question, "Where are you headed?" Alice says, "I don't know." The Cat says, "Then it won't matter which road you take." Some sermons are like that; they head everywhere and nowhere.

I have also experienced sermons that are long strings of quotations, one quotation after another. You can almost see the card file and the topical index on the pastor's desk. In more recent times, the pastor may sit at his computer, with the card file and index now stored therein. In preparing the sermon, the pastor pulls from here and there, crafting together a lengthy list of quotations, with some filler in between, that is then preached as the sermon of the morning.

On occasion, I have listened to sermons of fury. The preacher, in anger and admonition, in a furious kind of way, tries to scare and frighten the people toward some new direction. A few sermons are simply a barren desert, with no water for the week to come. A few are so much fluff and flimsy. It is so much cotton candy, froth, and fizz. Such sermons do not give people handles of help and hope.

Some sermons are managerial, preoccupied with policies and procedures, rules and regulations, conditions and stipulations. Some are institutional, concerned with saving the organization, or, at least, slowing down its withering decline. Some are apocalyptic, almost manufacturing one crisis after another. All of these are of lesser value. They have had their day.

It occurred to me recently that we have these fourteen types of preaching because we have people who are living these fourteen types of ways in their own lives. People preach the way they live. For example, an institutional person preaches institutional sermons. A teaching person preaches teaching, educational sermons.

What is helpful in our time, and likely in all times, are these five types of sermons from among the fourteen that are abroad:

A shepherding sermon
A motivational sermon
A teaching sermon
A missional sermon
An outcome sermon, a helping sermon

Mostly, congregations long to discover grace and compassion, peace and calm, hope and encouragement, wisdom and insight, for the week to come. People yearn to have this spirit *from both head and heart.* They value the sermons that are helpful in their lives.

In the helpful preaching of this time, in the outcome preaching of our day, we know this:

> People experience grace, peace, and hope.
> They discover wisdom and insight.
> Their emotions are stirred.
> Behavior moves forward.
> We live as whole, healthy persons in the grace of God.

Helpful preaching, outcome preaching makes a difference. People's lives are advanced.

On a given Sunday, the outcome focus of a sermon may be on grace. People, on that Sunday, experience the grace of God, the moving, stirring compassion and forgiving spirit of God in their lives. It is not that the sermon just talks about grace. People actually experience the grace of God. People are touched by the grace of God.

On another Sunday, the outcome focus may be on peace. People sense the peace of Christ in their lives. They experience calm and contentment. They are at peace. Their fear and anxiety are calmed. They are no longer afraid. They experience being at peace.

On another Sunday, the major outcome emphasis may be on hope. People experience the confidence and assurance, the encouragement and stirrings of hope in their lives. They experience the hope of God in their lives.

On yet another Sunday, the outcome focus may be on wisdom. People discover insights and wisdom, common sense and practical possibilities for their lives.

Outcomes

The primary outcome, the primary focus of a helping sermon, an outcome sermon, is on one of these four:

> Grace
> Peace
> Hope
> Wisdom

The other three will be present. These four helpful outcome focus points are in dynamic interaction with one another.

Be at peace about trying to focus on all four in a sermon. You do not need to do so. Focus on one helpful focus, one result, one outcome. The other three will be there, supporting and encouraging.

In a teaching sermon, the nature of the sermon is one of education and teaching. The sermon discusses the educational focus of the sermon. For example, in an educational sermon on peace, the sermon discusses some of the aspects of peace in relation to the scripture on peace. The spirit of the sermon is education.

In an outcome sermon, a helping sermon, people, as a result of the sermon, experience the event of peace in their lives. It is more than educational. It is fully experiential. People experience moments of peace.

Likewise, in an outcome sermon on hope, people experience living in hope during the sermon. It is more that educational. People experience the reality of hope amidst the sharing of the sermon.

Yes, I am using the term, "Helpful Preaching" in a technical spirit. In a broader sense, my hope is that all preaching is helpful preaching. Here, I am using the term in a more focused spirit. In this sense, helpful preaching focuses on a sermon whose direct outcome has to do with grace, peace, hope, or wisdom. People *experience* one of these four outcome gifts in their lives as a result of the sermon.

In a sense, helpful preaching is behavior preaching. It is good news preaching. It is parable preaching. The sermon shares just enough of the grace and compassion of God, just enough peace and calm of Christ, just enough handles of hope and help of the Holy Spirit, just enough in the way of wisdom and insight that people can discover, for themselves, the direction in which they plan to head as they live whole, healthy lives in the grace of God.

What is true of helpful preaching is true of helpful living.

When we live in the grace and compassion of God, in the peace and calm of Christ, in the hope and encouragement of the Holy Spirit, and in the wisdom and insights of a sacramental life, we now live in hope. We live helpful lives in grace, peace, and hope.

You are welcome, each day of your life, to focus on one of these four gifts.

Grace

Peace

Hope

Wisdom

You might decide, on a given day, to focus on grace. Live this day, fully, in the grace of God. Let the spirit of the day be one of grace and compassion. Share, on this day, with persons your gracious spirit of grace, compassion, and love.

On yet another day, intentionally decide to be a person of peace and calm, contentment and quiet. You will enjoy the day. People around you will enjoy the day.

Your life will have, for this day, a sense of well being and peace.

Likewise, select a day where you live in hope and the outcome, the result, will be hope. You will experience a spirit of confidence

Outcomes

and assurance on this day. You will move forward to a strong, healthy future. You will live in hope.

And, you can choose a day for wisdom and reflection, insight and common sense. This day, let your thoughtful and reflective gifts come to the fore. Let this not be a busy day with lots of projects to which one must give much attention. This can be a less busy, more reflective day. The outcome may be a deeper assessment of the direction in which one is heading.

The primary outcome, the primary focus of a given day in your life can be on one of these four:

> Grace
> Peace
> Hope
> Wisdom

The other three will be present. These four helpful focus points are in dynamic interaction with one another. Be at peace about trying to focus on all four in a given day. You do not need to do so. Focus on one helpful focus, one result, one outcome. The other three will be there, supporting and encouraging.

You can decide the night before on the one focus with which you will live on the day to come. As you begin the new day, focus on the outcome to which you look forward on this one day. At the end of the day, reflect on the extent to which you have fulfilled the focus for the day.

You lead your day, or your day leads you.

God blesses us with outcomes. God longs for our days to have positive outcomes. God yearns for our days to have constructive results. Live on the outcomes. You will live in hope.

A possibility for valuing the gift of hope with which God blesses you is to live for outcomes. God blesses you with outcomes, with results. Feel free to choose the focus of each day God gives to you. This intentional choice by you is more helpful than letting the day chose the focus for you. You lead your day. You head toward the results for which you hope. In doing so, you will live a day in hope.

God blesses you with outcomes. God blesses you with results.

God blesses us with the gift of outcomes so we can live in hope.

War and Hope

GOD BLESSES US WITH HOPE BEYOND WAR.

God blesses the universe with hope before the universe begins. God blesses the universe with hope as the universe begins. God blesses the universe with hope as the universe moves forward.

God blesses human kind with hope before war begins. God blesses humanity with hope even as war begins. God blesses humanity with hope during war, even during the blood and trenches, the machine guns and bombs, the sinking of ships, and the downing of planes. Amid the wounded and the dead, God seeks to share the gift of hope. God blesses us with hope beyond war.

God surrounds us with hope.

Julie's Great Grandfather fought in the War Between the States. He was captured in a bitter battle, placed in a newly and barely constructed war prison, and, a few months later, died in the cold of that bleak winter.

Julie's father fought in the Great War in the mud and trenches of France and Germany. This was a massive war, with new kinds of weapons and new kinds of deaths. Millions of soldiers, sailors, and airplane pilots covered the landscape. We now call that War World War I. He made it back home.

My father fought in the War in the Pacific. My uncle fought in the War in North Africa and Europe. For historical convenience, we lump these two massive wars together and call them World War II.

In fact, these are two very distinct wars, fought in very distinct ways. Each war should be referred to by its rightful name. For the Pacific war, it is rightfully called "The War in the Pacific." The wonderful War Museum in Fredericksburg, Texas, gives the war its proper name and is a fitting tribute.

The European war is rightfully and properly called "The War in North Africa and Europe." Each war was fought in its own distinct way and had its own distinctive consequences for all parties.

Both my father and my uncle made it back home. Julie's cousin, Rowena, did not. She was the first woman from Akron, Ohio to die in the war. She died in Hollandia.

As I write these words, as you read these words, we are aware of how frequently our lives are touched by war and hope.

Fear

War and Hope have something to do with fear. In John 14:27 we discover these words of Jesus,

> Peace I leave with you, my peace I give unto you: not as the world giveth, give I unto you. Let not your heart be troubled, neither let it be afraid.

Jesus' gift is not a Kingdom. It is not a Mission. It is not a Cause. Jesus' gift is peace. Jesus' understanding of the human predicament is fear. His gift is peace.

War and Hope

In the ancient Upanishads, there is a mantra:

> Sow a thought
> Reap an action
> Sow an action
> Reap a habit
> Sow a habit
> Reap a character
> Sow a character
> Reap a destiny

In a somewhat similar spirit, I wrote this mantra several years ago:

> Fear breeds anxiety
> Fear and anxiety breed anger
> Fear, anxiety, and anger breed rage
> Fear, anxiety, anger, and rage breed war
> War breeds death, despair, and destruction
> Fear is the heart of the human predicament.

The search for greed and the longing for power are human efforts to overcome fear. People vainly seek money and greed, domination and power to still, to quiet their innate fear. People go to war to still their fear.

On May 3, 1915, Colonel John McCrae, a Canadian physician, after presiding over the funeral of friend and fellow soldier Alexis Helmer, who died in the Second Battle of Ypres, wrote the war poem, **In Flanders Fields.**

Red poppies grew over the graves of slain soldiers. The poem and the poppy have become among the most recognized signs of soldiers who have fallen in battle.

> In Flanders fields the poppies blow
> Between the crosses, row on row
> That mark our place; and in the sky
> The larks, still bravely, singing, fly
> Scarce heard amid the guns below.
>
> We are the Dead. Short days ago
> We lived, felt dawn, saw sunset glow,
> Loved and were loved, and now we lie
> In Flanders fields.
>
> Take up our quarrel with the foe:
> To you from failing hands we throw
> The torch; be yours to hold it high.
> If ye break faith with us who die
> We shall not sleep, though poppies grow
> In Flanders fields.

When we find fear, we find war. When we find war, we find death. When we find death and despair, we long for hope. When we find war, we find hope.

Power

War is about power:

> Monarchies, republics, democracies,
> Industrialism, trade, raw materials, raw commodities,
> Greed, consumption, and power.

Yes, human kind blunders into some of its wars. These wars come about because some one or some ones make one or more blundering, stupid mistakes that lead to a dismal, obtuse war.

Most of humanity's wars are more intentional.

War and Hope

Monarchies, republics, and democracies battle for power, lands, and oceans. Nations fight over industrialism and trade, raw materials and raw commodities. Greed and wealth, status and prestige, and domination and hierarchy lead whole peoples to war.

West and Eastman, in their classic work, **World Progress**, suggest,

"Modern civilization is based upon industrialism. Now the life blood of industrialism is trade: trade not merely with civilized nations, but also with tropical and subtropical countries for oil, rubber, ivory, minerals, and other raw materials needed by factories in civilized lands.

Moreover, thanks to modern factory processes, every industrial country (which can get adequate supplies of raw materials) has a much greater output than its own people can buy. The factories cannot keep running full speed without outside markets in which to sell.

In the industrial states, too (before the World War), wealth accumulated faster, at times, than it could be invested profitably, - so that capitalists were anxious for outside investments, especially in countries with naturally rich but as yet undeveloped resources."

Their analysis is helpful. They are writing in 1936, some years after the Great War. Humanity had hardly seen a war as horrific as the one through which they had recently been.

Underlying their analysis of industrialism and trade is a deeper matter. Human kind tends to go to war whenever these five steps take place. I call these the five steps to war:

1. Fear
2. Anxiety
3. Anger
4. Rage
5. Power

These five steps to war begin with fear. The lust for power is a way some people try to lessen their originating fear. Strong fear leads to strong lust for power in an effort to overcome fear.

Yes, the propensity of humanity to war is an ever present threat to hope.

Christ's gift of peace is the antidote to war. Where there is grace, peace, and hope, there is no war. Where there is fear, anxiety, and anger, there is a propensity to war.

Edmund Burke once wrote, "Tyranny is a weed that grows on all soils, and it is its nature to spread. As a companion to his sentiment, Kennon Callahan, yours truly, once wrote, "Democracy is the flower that grows in all gardens, and it is its nature to bloom and spread."

Willis M. West and S. Mack Eastman end their monumental work, *World Progress*, with these words,

> "Nevertheless, the year 1935 ended perilously rather than gloomily, for the gloom was relieved now and then by a gleam of hope."

Their book is published in 1936. The Great War is behind. The League of Nations is in the midst of a faltering existence. There is no full grasp of what is to come.

My thought is that this gleam, this glimpse, this meager ray of hope may be all that we can count on and hope for in the decades before us.

Grassroots

A puzzle of our time is the source of power.

In an earlier time, Klemens von Metternich (1773-1859) wrote,

> "Sovereigns alone are entitled to guide the destinies of their peoples, and they are responsible to none

but God. Government is no more a subject for debate than religion is. The new ideas of democracy and equality and nationality ought never to have been allowed to get into Europe, but, since they were in, the business of government must be to keep them down."

At his coronation, William I of Germany (1797-1888) wanted to confirm the Divine Right of Emperors. He took the crown from the communion table, declaring, "The crown comes only from God, and I have received it from His hands."

In 1815, when Louis XVIII becomes king of France, the original Divine-Right Monarchy in France is downgraded to a Constitutional Kingship. He knew that the people must have some assurance of those personal liberties which they had won in the Revolution. Accordingly, he gave to the nation the Charter of 1815.

I observe that this action of Louis XVIII comes just nearly 300 years after 1517 when Luther posts his 95 Theses, declaring that the Grace of God comes equally to all persons. God's grace does not come in a hierarchical, top down, descending way to Pope, Council, Cardinals, Archbishops, Bishops, Priests, and, finally, to people.

The Pharaohs held sway for 3,200 years. Emperors, Kings, and Dictators held court for centuries, in Rome, Europe, Russia, England, and across the planet. Slowly and gradually, it has come to be that power is seen, more and more, to be grassroots, not top down.

This struggle between monarchs and grassroots has gone on for a long, long time. Monarchs have depended on a hierarchy of God's grace to buttress their own positions of power. The notion that God's grace came, in a top down fashion, first to Popes and Kings, gave a false credence to the notion that power is top down.

But, when grace comes from God directly and equally to all persons; then, power is not top town. Power is in the grassroots. Slowly and certainly, humanity is coming to this understanding. Grace is grassroots. Power is grassroots.

War

The causes of war are many.

> Fear, Power, and Greed
> Top Down and Grassroots Understandings of Life
> Industrialization
> Computerization
> The War Tradition
> The self-mutilation of humanity

Fear, Power, and Greed.

The beginnings of war have something to do with fear. Fear is an ever present dilemma for human kind. Fear becomes anxiety. Anxiety becomes anger. Anger turns into rage. Rage becomes the search for power and greed to overcome the originating fear, and we now have war.

The illusion is that power and greed will provide stability and security to overcome the originating sense of fear. When we have enough power and enough wealth, we will stabilize our fear. The puzzle is that power and greed are temporary, momentary efforts to deal with fear. They do not last.

Top Down and Grassroots Understandings of Life.

Yes, and we have massive battles between top down and grassroots understandings of how to order life. These disputes between monarchies and democracies have been long standing sources of wars in humanity. Gods have been invoked to bolster the on-going disputes.

The puzzle is how does one best order the day to day lives of people so they can live whole, healthy lives. The emerging answer is that grassroots possibilities provide the most helpful way forward. Grace is grassroots. Power is grassroots. Life is grassroots. Hope is grassroots.

Industrialization.

Industrialization has contributed its fair share to the development of wars in recent times. The competition for raw materials across the globe has been a major factor. The struggle for manufacturing centers and for viable markets has added to the dilemma.

Computerization.

The new Age of Computerization adds a deeper dimension to the developing dynamic of war. We have entered a new realm that humanity has not experienced in previous times.

The War Tradition.

In *World Progress*, West and Eastman give mention to the war tradition in the course of human history. On page 702, they write:

> Among the fundamental causes of the catastrophe of August, 1914, must be reckoned the persistence of the war-tradition in human society.
>
> Difficulties between peoples had nearly always been referred to the supreme arbitrament of the sword, and the presumption among rulers and foreign offices and general staffs was that only "Utopians" talked of the suppression of war.
>
> Prose and poetry glorified the field of battle, and children were nurtured in the worship of military

heroes. Furthermore, nations had come to be personified and idealized, so that even crassly material disputes between opposing vested interests, backed by their respective governments, were often exalted in popular imagination to the level of romantic or heroic duels between, let us say, "Austria" and "Russia," or "France" and Germany."

West and Eastman observe that on April 6, 1917, the United States declared war and mobilized 9, 500, 000 troops through conscription. By June 6, troops are arriving in France, and by September they would infallibly tip the balance in favor of the Allies.

The Great War is a massive illustration of the war tradition.

The notion of a war tradition in the nature of humanity is an interesting possibility. West and Eastman have an interesting suggestion. Certainly, there is ample evidence of such a possibility across the centuries of civilization.

Might there also be a "peace tradition." One would hope so.

The self-mutilation of humanity. A sixth contributing factor to war is what West and Eastman refer to as the self-mutilation of humanity. On page 721 of <u>World Progress</u>, they write,

> Once More Mars Stalked Abroad. – During the days succeeding the outbreak to war (The Great War), an observer from the stratosphere might have fancied he was witnessing a vast migration of peoples. Millions of men were on the march, recalling the days of the Goths, Vandals, and Huns.
>
> However, apart from the dire significance of their marching, there the semblance ended.

War and Hope

> In 1914, the never-ending columns were moving in machine-made uniforms and equipment, with scientific precision, according to minutely prepared schedules, accompanied by mechanical transport, armed with such deadly weapons as earlier generations had never dreamed of, guided by signals from the air and invisible messages through the ether.
>
> They represented the mobilization of all the powers of Man, - mental and physical, - and all the resources of Nature – for the self-mutilation of the human race."

Yes, I resist the notion that humanity has a built-in predisposition for self-mutilation. And, at times, it seems that predilection, that propensity is present. Perhaps, the originating fear within humanity and the tendency to self-mutilation have something in common.

West and Eastman, on page 125, note, the age of Pericles saw also a rapid development in philosophy, - and this movement, too, had Athens for its most important home. Anaxagoras of Ionia, the friend of Pericles, taught that the ruling principle in the universe was Mind: "In the beginning all things were chaos; then came intelligence, and set all in order."

I would humbly suggest, "In the beginning, was grace, and then came peace, and then hope, then came heart, and set all things to loving. Heart sets things to loving, and then mind sets things to order. Heart is before mind. We are a people of heart. The universe is a matter of heart."

The dynamic of war and the gift of hope have a common bond. Where we find war, we also tend to find hope.

A possibility in coming to understand the gift of hope with which God blesses you is to understand the dynamic of war and

hope. War is sufficiently present in the lives of human kind that it becomes important to develop a sense of the relationship of war and hope.

Some persons seem to have a propensity for war. Many persons have a longing for peace. Feel free to live your hope. Build on your strengths and your motivation. Focus not on your weaknesses and shortcomings. To do so would only lead to fear and war.

Hope steadies us. We have less fear. We worry less. We are less anxious. We can move beyond doubt. We can move beyond despair. We can live in the grace, peace, and hope of God.

God gives us the gift of hope with which we can move beyond war.

Hope

GOD BLESSES US WITH THE WONDERS, POWER, AND JOY OF HOPE.

Before the Beginning

God is. God is before. God is before the beginning. Before the beginning, there is God. Before the universe, there is God.

God is before the beginning. More precisely, before the universe begins, there is grace, peace, and hope. Wherever and whenever God is, there is grace, peace, and hope.

The grace of God, the peace of Christ, and the Hope of the Holy Spirit are the earliest, first gifts even before the beginning.

Grace and compassion, peace and calm, and hope and encouragement are the gifts with which God blesses us. Religion and science are man's efforts, man's constructs to understand life, reality, and God.

God is God.

God is not religion or science. These are man's creations. Likewise, philosophy, math, physics....these are ways we seek to give some meaning and significance to our existence.

The universe is the living creation, the living testimony to the grace, peace, and hope of God. The suns and the stars, the galaxies and the comets, and the light years and the dark holes are signs of the grace, peace, and hope of God.

God is God.

> "'For I know the plans I have for you,' declares the Lord, 'plans to prosper you and not to harm you, plans to give you hope and a future'"
>
> Jeremiah 29:11

God gives us the gift of hope. This gift of hope is even before the beginning.

The Wonders of Hope

Hope is extraordinary in our lives. The nature of hope is remarkable. The qualities of hope, the wonders of hope give it special significance in our lives. Hope is:

> Active and moving
> Creative and joyful
> Independent and energetic
> Strong and vigorous
> Calm and stirring
> Realistic and concrete
> The gift of God

Hope is ***active and moving***, not passive, wishful thinking. Wishful thinking is not hope. It is simply wishful thinking. It waits. It lingers. It stays. Wishful thinking remains still and waits on someone else to do something.

Hope moves. Hope is active. Hope takes initiative. Hope is proactive. Hope has a sense of direction. Hope has movement.

Hope is ***creative and joyful***, not sad and syrupy. Hope is original and imaginative. Hope has the spirit of being inventive and innovative. Some imagine that sadness passes for hope, that a thick, sugary sweetness passes for hope. Not so.

Hope is rich in creativity, vibrant with joy. Hope sings. Hope dances.

Hope is **independent and energetic**, not co-dependent – dependent. Hope has the spirit of self-reliance and resilience about it. There is no hope in co-dependent and dependent relationships. Such relationships have the fashion of a prison about them. It is never clear who is the more trapped.... the co-dependent.... or the dependent.

Hope lives in the open, fresh air of freedom and liberty. Hope has no chains. Hope stirs the individuality and spontaneity of persons.

Hope is **strong and vigorous**, not weak and wimpy. Indeed, the three good friends of grace, peace, and hope are the most dynamic and spirited forces in the universe. Hope is not frail and feeble, fragile and weedy. Hope stands strong and tall, giving a vigorous spirit to human kind.

Hope is **calm and stirring**, not angry and depressed. People who allow themselves to become angry and depressed lose hope. Note well. When we allow ourselves to become angry, we will become depressed. Depression is anger turned within. Anger and depression are twin dilemmas. They go together.

When we stay calm, we can allow our spirit of hope to stir and soar. Anger and depression distract us from the gift of hope with which God blesses us.

Hope is **realistic and concrete**, not false hope. Hope is specific and concrete, realistic and achievable. Hope is not false hope, vague and mythical, cloudy and foggy.

Feel free to stay away from false hope. Such fabrications do not help. They damage credibility and integrity. They break trust and respect.

Hope does not include the notion of "more." "More" is a never ending horizon of failure. We can never achieve a horizon of "more." Note well. "More" is a never ending horizon of failure. "More" is always one more over the horizon.

Hope builds trust when it is realistic. Hope advances credibility when it is concrete. Hope lasts and endures when it has this quality of respect.

Hope is ***the gift of God***.
Yes, Hope is
> *Active and moving,*
> *Creative and joyful,*
> *Independent and energetic,*
> *Strong and vigorous,*
> *Calm and stirring,*
> *Realistic and concrete,*

and, most important of all, the seventh quality of Hope is:

Hope is the gift of God.

The first six qualities are active qualities. These six qualities confirm that you and I actively participate in Hope. God intends that we are active participants in the Spirit of Hope. The seventh quality confirms and reconfirms that we do so as gift of God.

Our active participation in Hope might lead us to the minor temptation that we are, in part at least, an author of Hope. The primary source of Hope, confirmed in the seventh quality, is God. The gift of Hope, the wonder of Hope, is that Hope is the gift of God.

The Power of Hope

Someone once said,

"To me, hope is the last resort. It is what you hang on to, when everything else has failed. Try every other possibility first. Hope is the last thing you hang on to when nothing else has worked."

My response was,

"To me, hope is the first resort. It is what you begin with so everything else will work. Hope is the first thing you begin with so everything else will work."

Hope is God's gift. Hope is not audacity. Some share power. Some keep power. Some build power. Hope is you taking care of yourself. Hope is not some one else taking care of you. Hope is self-reliance. Hope is God-reliance.

Four possibilities are available to us:

1. There is always hope.
2. There is sometimes hope.
3. There is now and then hope.
4. There is never hope.

In the course of a day, a week, a month we may live each of these four. We may move from one to another.

The gift of God is the first one. *"There is always hope."* We manufacture the other three. The other three are constructs we invent to give us solace in this life, to excuse our occasional discouragement and despair.

Sometimes, I think God allows us to know of the other 3 so we will cherish the first one, God's gift, even more so. Yes, be of good cheer. Take heart. There is always hope. There is always God.

Hope is not for the weak, the foolish, the lazy, the indifferent, the stick in the muds, the hysterical, the overly anxious, the ones who are brimming over with excuses.

The most decisive understanding of God in the Old Testament is of the God who goes before the People as a cloud by day and a fire by night, leading them to that future which God has promised and is preparing for them.

Our God is not like the old gods of that ancient time. If our God had been like those old gods, he would have said, once on the safe side of the Red Sea, "You all build a Temple for me here by the safe side of the Red Sea. The view is beautiful. It is quiet. I will stay here in comfort and peace.

The future is out there somewhere in that desert. You all head on out. See what you can find. I know it is out there, some where…. the future. And, should you get tired, or lonely, or discouraged, or hungry, you come on back and we will figure out a new plan."

Our God is not a God of the past. Our God is the God of the Future. Our God is the active, moving into the future God. Our God is the God of the Promised Land.

The most decisive understanding of God in the New Testament is the God of the Open Tomb, the Risen Lord, and new life in Christ. Our God is the God of the Future. Our God is the God of Hope. Our God goes before us into that New Life, leading us to our New Future. The power of Hope is that it is God's gift, the gift of the future, the gift of new life.

The Joy of Hope

People discover the joy of hope. People live on the joy of hope. The joy of hope stirs people to action. When we are experiencing the joy of hope, we move forward in action. When people are having fun, they stir themselves to movement.

Wishful thinking is not a strategy. Wishful thinking goes nowhere. Wishful thinking does not mobilize a person or a group. Wishful thinking causes a person to wait, to do nothing, to sit, to look for someone else to do something. There is no hope in the waiting. There is no joy in the waiting.

Hope is none of the following:

> Hope is not wishful thinking.
> Hope is not false hope.
> Hope is not compulsive hope.
> Hope is not abusive hope.
> Hope is not a strategy.
> Hope is not a last resort

There is no joy in any of these six. There is no joyful spirit in any of these six. Each of these six sometimes parades as though they were hope. They are a poor imitation of the qualities, power, and joy of God's gift of hope in your life.

God comforts us. God does not make all things comfortable. The gift of hope is in the joy, comfort, and assurance of hope, not in everything being comfortable.

Hope is confident expectancy and joyful assurance. Hope happens with grace and peace. There is a joy in the song that grace, peace, and hope sing in our lives.

Hope is the sweetness of a spring rain gently falling to bring new life to a weary winter world. Hope is the sound of the bugle, far off, bringing hope. The lost fight has been saved. Hope is the rise of the wind so we can set sail. We sail before the storm.

Hope is a quiet conversation of encouragement. Hope is the gentle dawn of a new day. Hope overcomes hopelessness.

A possibility for understanding the gift of hope with which God blesses you is to value the wonders, power, and joy of the generous gift of Hope.

Hope overcomes discouragement, despondency, depression, despair. Discouragement is the beginning of despondency is the beginning of depression is the beginning of despair. Hope is God's gift amidst all of that.

In the birth of Jesus, the three wise men bring the gifts of gold, frankincense, and mir. I think the three wise men bring the gifts of grace, peace, and hope. There is much joy. The manger is filled with happiness and gladness. A new child has been born.

In the parable of the Running Father, sometimes called the parable of the Prodigal Son, we discover the father does not wait in the house. While his young son is yet a long way off, the Father sees his young son, and runs to his son, throws his arms around him, and welcomes him home. He calls for the cloak of grace, the ring of peace, and the sandals of hope. There is much joy.

Much in life is spontaneous. Some of life is planned. We know where we are headed and we have a thoughtful plan for moving forward. And, much of life happens with a spontaneous spirit.

> Spontaneous grace overcomes selfishness and doubt.
> Spontaneous peace overcomes anxiety, fear, anger, rage.
> Spontaneous hope overcomes doubt, dread, depression, despair.

Hope is mostly spontaneous, not planned. Too much planning delays, defeats hope. Sometimes, our planning is so elaborate and careful that the planning takes the joy out of the hope. Do just enough planning that we have some sense of where we are headed but not so much planning that we lose the joy of hope.

Home is hope….hope is home. Where we find home, we discover hope. Where we find hope, we discover home. There is much joy.

Audrey Hepburn once wrote, "Nothing is impossible. The word itself says, "I'm possible." We discover much joy when we live life with the spirit of hope, with the spirit of what is possible.

With fear, we sink. With hope, we walk. Hope is willing. Fear is weak. With hope, we discover joy.

There are three Sacraments.

> The Sacrament of Grace celebrates the Birth in the Manger.
> The Sacrament of Peace celebrates the Supper in the Upper Room.
> The Sacrament of Hope celebrates the Open Tomb, the Risen Lord, and New Life.

It is said that the way to hell is paved with good intentions. I say to you that the way to heaven is paved with grace, peace, and hope. There is much joy by living in hope.

Live with a strong sense of grace, peace, and hope. We believe we are worthy of being loved and belonging. We believe we are worthy of loving and growing. We live a whole-hearted life, moving forward in this life.

God blesses you with the wonders, power, and joy of hope.

Cast Your Nets

GOD BLESSES YOU WITH NETS.

God blesses you with nets. Cast your nets. You will live in hope.

Peter was standing on the shore. He did not know what to do next. He said, "Well, I guess I'll go back to fishing."

Some of the disciples were there with him. They did not know what to do next either. They said, "Well, we guess we'll go with you."

Old ways die hard.

There had been three rich, full years with Christ. The teachings, the miracles, the crowds, the times away, the wonders, the gentle, quiet times. There had been Palm Sunday, Upper Room, Gethsemane, Golgotha, Cross, Death, Hiding. Then, there had been Open Tomb, Resurrection, Risen Lord, and New Life.

With all the wonder and joy, all the new hope and new life of those amazing three years and their experiences with their risen Lord, they did not now know what to do next. They went back to the old ways.

They went out fishing all night.

They tried all their favorite fishing places: over there, and over there, over there, almost desperately they tried yet over there. "We used to catch fish here about 2:00 in the morning." They used to catch fish in all these places, but they were catching no fish all night long.

Their boat was not empty. Their boat was filling with despair, depression, discouragement, and despondency early that morning. None of the places where they used to catch fish worked. They had been good fishermen, and they were catching nothing all that night.

Not even the old ways worked anymore.

Early that morning, sunrise dawning, they were headed to shore. Tired. Worn. Discouraged. Forlorn.

A stranger was standing on the shore. The setting is very clear. The stranger is Jesus.

And they do not know that it is Jesus.

The stranger hollers out, "Have you caught any fish?"

Now, what would any good fisherman known for making a living at catching fish—yea, even a recreational fisherman – usually say?

"Yes."

"And the fish are getting even bigger and bigger each time we tell our tales."

But this time, there is an almost plaintive plea, a quiet moan – you can almost hear the despair in the answer:

"No, we haven't caught any fish."

The stranger says, "Cast your nets on the starboard side of the boat."

Now, someone might suggest that the point is that we have been living too long with older patterns of behavior and that Christ now invites us to grow forward in fresh, new ways. Someone might suggest that. Surely not yours truly. And this is not the key point.

The key point of the text, the miracle of the story, is in the words,

"And they did."

We sometimes think the miracle is that the nets are now so loaded with fish that the fishermen can hardly bring them into the boat. This is the second miracle. The first miracle is in the words, "And they did."

You see, this is a stranger on the shore. All they know is that a stranger has invited them to cast their nets on the other side of the boat. All they know is how tired they are. All they know is they want to get to shore.

The miracle is "And they did."

What could they have done?

> They could have said they had already tried that.
> They could have held a committee meeting.
> They could have had a long, lengthy discussion.
> They could have developed a ninety-seven page, long-range plan for fishing for the coming ten years.
> Ah, they could have rowed the other way.

The miracle is,
> ***even when Jesus comes to us as a stranger,***
> ***we discover new ways in Christ.***

Yes, old ways die hard. Yes, we do discover new ways in Christ. We grow and learn. We develop and build. We discover hope.

The second miracle is that the nets are so loaded with fish they can hardly get them in the boat.

The third miracle is in the words, "It is the Lord." It is only after casting their nets at the invitation of a stranger that they discover the stranger is Jesus.

What we learn from these words is this:

> Cast your nets, you will see Christ.

It is not that we discover Christ and then go and do the mission. It is in the sharing of the mission that we discover Christ. It is in serving people with grace and peace and hope that we discover Jesus.

Remember what the angel says to the women,

> "And tell the disciples that Christ has gone before them into Galilee."

Christ has gone before them into the new life and mission. It is not that first we grow ourselves forward and *then* we go share in the mission. It is in the sharing of the mission that we grow forward. It is in serving people with their human hurts and hopes that we discover Christ.

Where is Christ? Christ lives and dies and is risen again and again among the human hurts and hopes of the people God has planted all around us. This is where Christ is. This is where God is.

A possibility for growing your the gift of hope with which God blesses you is to cast your nets.

There is a fourth miracle. A wondrous miracle.

As the boat gets to shore, Jesus says to the disciples,

> "Come and have breakfast."

We learn this from the text: Christ cares for our every need.

Christ understands the disciples have been fishing all night long. The old ways have not worked. They are tired and hungry.

There is no long lecture. There is no lengthy list of commandments. There is no "Why haven't you figured it out in the past three years?"

There is simply, "Come, breakfast is ready."

Count on – depend on – this. God cares for your every need.

May God's blessings of growing and developing, grace and peace, hope and new life be ever with you and yours. God bless you. God be with you. Come. Your new life is ready

God blesses you with nets. Cast your nets.

It is not that we find hope, and, then, cast our nets.
It is in the casting of our nets that we discover hope.
Cast your nets. Live in hope.

Gossip, Apathy, Generations

GOSSIP, APATHY, GENERATIONS

Gossip

Guilt breeds grudge. Grudge breeds gossip. The way beyond guilt is to accept the forgiveness of God and to forgive ourselves. These two help us beyond the guilt. It is clear that, without accepting the forgiving grace of God, we allow the guilt to become a latent grudge, and the latent grudge leads us to the practice of gossip.

Gossip is the practice of trying to distract ourselves both from our guilt and our refusing to accept God's forgiveness and our own forgiveness. Instead, gossips spend time pointing to someone else's guilt to overcompensate for their own.

Gossips gossip.

People who make demeaning comments about one person make demeaning comments about others. They almost do not realize they have developed the habit of gossip. It is virtually automatic. The language of gossip is so much a pattern for them that they barely know they do it.

Gossip is the denial of hope.

When you gossip you take away hope. You place your trust in what is not true,

And you cut yourself off from your true and promising future. You cut yourself off from hope.

Be not a listener of gossip.

Two reasons. One, when you listen to gossip you reinforce the gossiper in his or her pattern of gossip. You encourage them to be even more a dispenser of gossip. Two, and even more dangerous, when you listen to gossip, you might pick up the disease and you, yourself, might become a gossip.

When you participate in gossip, as practitioner or listener or both, you encourage the habit in the gossiper and in yourself. You reinforce the notion that gossip is an idle and innocent past time. Gossip is not idle and innocent. Gossip is dangerous and dreadful.

When I suggest gossip is dreadful I am not being harsh. Gossip is appalling because gossip seeks to diminish hope. Gossip puts people down. Gossip does not lift up. Gossip tells half truths, untruths, distortions, lies, and falsehoods. Gossip is not innocent.

Listen not to gossip.

Gossip is not your friend.

Gossip pulls you down, and pulls down the person saying it. You can also wonder and be as concerned for what the gossiper is saying to someone else about you. Gossipers say something about some one to you. They are as likely to gossip about you to someone else.

When you listen to gossip, you will be talked about in gossip. When you join gossip as a listener, you passively agree to become the subject of gossip in some other conversation. You can always wonder what your gossiper friend is saying.... is saying.... is saying about you.

Gossip gallops.

Gossip is not grace.

Fortunately, persons are not born as gossips. They learn to become gossips from other well practiced gossipers. If you have allowed yourself to become a gossiper, ask yourself from whom you learned the pattern of gossip. It may be more than one person. Now, ask yourself from whom you can learn to no longer be a gossip.

Being a gossip is a learned pattern of behavior. One can learn to not be a gossip. Gossip is an addiction. People learn to move beyond many forms of addiction. Select your mentor and coach who will be of wondrous help to you to give up gossip.

Gossip demeans. When you demean someone, you demean yourself. When we gossip, we fall into the double trap of demeaning and placating pleasing. These two are friends. Persons sense, in their gossip, that they are demeaning persons, and they try to compensate by placating pleasing other persons.

Peace is peace.

Placating pleasing is not peace. On occasion, pleasing may lead to peace.

Mostly, placating pleasing may just lead to the demand for more pleasing, and no peace.

Yes, you are encouraged to please persons, when the pleasing has its own integrity and worth.

Pleasing is not peace. Pleasing is not a solution to strife, upsetness, anger, and frustration. Placating pleasing is not, does not, will not lead to peace. Placating pleasing just leads to more placating pleasing. There is no end. Placating pleasing is a never-ending, always one more over the horizon placating pleasing. It never ends.

There is no hope in gossip.

There is no hope in demeaning.

There is no hope in placating pleasing.

Gossip damages persons and groupings reputations and integrity. Worse, yet even worse, gossip seeks to destroy hope. Gossip seeks to harm hope. Gossip does not do hope in. Hope is stronger than that.

Think about it. Have you ever heard a bit of gossip that was hopeful, that encouraged the spirit of hope. Most forms of gossip are negative, harmful, spiteful, putting someone down. Gossip discourages hope.

When someone begins to share gossip with you, the best way forward is to say,

> "Let's discuss something else. I am not interested in that subject."

And, then, move on to a subject that encourages hope.

Even more helpful, be not a person who starts gossip. Be not a person who starts even tiny forms of gossip. Be a person who encourages strong hope.

Apathy

Apathy may indeed be apathy. People learn apathy as a pattern of behavior.

The pattern serves them well. Apathy serves the function of helping persons to not be scared or scarred yet again in their lives. Persons become frightened by some event or series of events. Or, they become abused in some way by some person or persons. Or, both happen.

A retreat to apathy becomes an avoidance pattern to stay away from being scared or scarred yet again. And apathy frequently fulfills this function well, and, so long as this function continues to keep one away from being scared or scarred, apathy tends to be a pattern of behavior.

The puzzle is this: apathy tends to diminish hope. More accurately put, apathy distracts us from God's gift of hope. Whatever events or persons have scared or scarred us, God's gift of hope is a richer and fuller way of dealing with those events or persons.

Apathy is a lesser, poorer way of dealing with them.

Sometimes, we convince ourselves we are not worthy of God's gift of hope and we settle for a lesser way. Our low self esteem gets in the way. Apathy becomes our bed fellow. Yes, instead, we can choose the hope of God.

Discover a mentor or coach who can walk with you as you move from apathy to hope as a way of life.

Now, apathy is most likely a sign, a symptom of one of these:

1. **A mismatch of motivations.** Think of six motivations:

    compassion
    community
    hope
    challenge
    reasonability
    commitment

    The leaders' primary motivation is challenge. The grass roots' primary motivation is compassion. The leaders and the group live on very different motivational wave lengths. The group's behavior will appear as apathy. In reality, it is a motivational mismatch, a motivational gap.

2. **Lack of ownership.** When people are included in deciding the way forward, they participate in achieving the project. Many times people are not included in shaping the project, and so they do not participate in achieving the project. This is not apa-

thy. They are teaching us they lack ownership for the project.

3. **Strengths.** They sense that their strengths may not match the task at hand. They back off from the project to teach us they sense this mismatch. People prefer to not do projects for which they do not have reasonable strengths. This in not apathy. This is common sense.

4. **History.** Some persons and groupings have a history of turmoil, perfectionism, and being stuck. The turmoil happens in a series of events that are chaotic and confusing, tragic and catastrophic. A compulsive addictive perfectionism is present. The person or the grouping gets "stuck." This is my term for what happens. The person or grouping becomes frozen in the turmoil. This is more than apathy. They have allowed the tragic events to paralyze their behavior.

5. **The lack of positive reinforcement.** It is not always the presence of negative reinforcement. Yes, it certainly could be. Negative reinforcement looks like the symptoms of apathy. Nay saying groups appear to look like apathetic groups. They are worse off. And, groupings that press negative reinforcement and lack positive reinforcement are even worse off.

Positive reinforcement stirs more movement any day than negative reinforcement every day. "Well done" are two of the most helpful and hopeful words in human kind.

6. **A culture mismatch.** In life, there are a variety of culture groupings.

   Some culture groupings, some common interest groupings are:

   > Athletic
   > Intellectual
   > Extracurricular
   > Social
   > Music
   > Arts
   > Computer
   > Fad
   > Outcast
   > Independents

   There are many more culture groupings. Some people in a given culture grouping simply do not have an interest in some of the activities of another culture grouping. They express their disinterest by not participating. It is not apathy. It is disinterest.

7. **Vocational mismatch.** There is a vast array of vocations on the planet. People tend to be drawn the vocation or vocations in which they have primary interest. And, vocational groupings, in larger fashion, tend to group as:

   > Worker
   > Manager
   > Owner
   > Entrepreneur

These larger groupings do various specific projects together. And, importantly, each larger grouping has distinctive projects they do separately. Sometimes, what some think of as apathy is really honoring the value of these distinctive projects.

8. **This is not a 20%.** The priority principle is:

    20% of our objectives yield 80% of our results.
    80% of our objectives yield 20% of our results.

    For many persons, they are glad to help with a 20% project. A key 20% project stirs their creativity and energy. They are not drawn to participate in a lesser project. It is not apathy that they are teaching us. They are teaching us their capacity to develop priorities primarily for key projects.

9. **Defeat, despair, depression.** Some persons, some groupings learn a pattern of defeat, despair, and depression. They develop the mentality of a "loosing team." They reinforce the perspective of "stable and declining and dying." They struggle to not lose any more than they have already lost. This is more than apathy.

10. **Compulsive addictive perfectionism.** Some persons, some groupings learn this pattern of behavior. There are many, many constructive groups across the planet who help persons live beyond this addictive pattern of behavior. For some, this destructive pattern creates the illusion of apathy. It is more.

Ask yourself, which of these ten possibilities contribute, in a given instance, to the perceived pattern of apathy? Two or three of these ten may contribute to the person or grouping's pattern of behavior.

Actually, we are dealing with eleven possibilities: apathy in its own right, and the ten listed above. Each has its own integrity. Each is worthy of consideration. Each of these eleven seeks to be an assassin of hope. Hope is stronger. And, two or three of these together can cause a person or a group to lose their spirit of hope.

The gift of God is Hope. Hope is God's gift to help you beyond each of these. You can assess which, if any, of these are contributing to a diminishing of hope in your life.

Generations

God encourages us to the growth of grace. God encourages us to the growth of peace. God encourages us to the growth of hope.

God is much less interested in something called church growth. Indeed, sometimes I think the notion of church growth is the devil's device to distract us from growing the grace, peace, and hope of God. I am confident that when we focus on growing grace, peace, and hope the puzzle of church growth will care for its self.

Mister Eckart has been known to say, "The devil has a devise called business with which he tries to convince Christians they are really doing the will of God." The distraction actually distracts Christians from doing the will of God.

As we think of the generations which come and go, we can know this:

1. The source of hope is the same for each generation. Hope is the gift of God. Hope is not something conjured up by human kind. It is not some vague feeling that we manufacture.

   Hope is the concrete and realistic gift of God.

2. Each generation develops each own distinctive stages of hope.

   The events of the times contribute to the ways in which hope lives forward with each generation. For an earlier generation, these stages happened:

   > The New Century, 1900
   > The Great War, now called World War I
   > The Roaring Twenties
   > The Depression
   > The War in the Pacific, now linked as World War II
   > The War in Africa and Europe, World War II
   > The Rebuilding of Civilization
   > Retirement
   > Growing Old Together

   These events shaped the stages of hope for a given generation. As new events come along, each generation develops each own stages of hope.

3. The dynamics of hope act both sequentially and simultaneously. Hope lives forward in sequential patterns, and hope has a simultaneous spirit of movement. Hope has the joy and creativity of being the moving force in the universe.

4. Generations do not live in isolation from one another. A grand parent generation and a grand child generation frequently reach, serve, and help one another. Power passes from one generation to,

not always the next generation. Power may pass to the next next or the next, next, next generation.

Persons who, now, are grandparents tend not to have passed the power to the next generation. They keep the power. They tend to pass the power to the next next generation, or even the next, next, next generation.

In our time, this seems to suggest the baby boomers are passing the power to the millennials. The sixty million are passing the power to the eighty million.

A possibility for growing the gift of hope with which God blesses you is to understand gossip, apathy, and generations.

Gossip seeks to diminish hope. Thus, we do not participate in gossip.

Apathy is more than apathy. There are eleven possibilities that seek to lessen the gift of hope. We discover ways to help the eleven not diminish the hope with which God blesses us.

Each generation discovers the stages of hope that match with the events of that generation. God seeks to match the gift of hope with the events of the times. God invites each generation to live with hope helpful to the times.

We know this.

Hope will take on the nature and focus helpful for the times to come. Hope is the gift of God. The nature and focus of hope resonates with the times with which God blesses us. God goes before us, as cloud by day and fire by night, leading us to the future which God is promising and preparing for us.

God's gift of hope overcomes gossip and apathy and helps each generation with the stages of hope that match with the events of their times.

Always

ALWAYS

There is always Hope.

There is always Hope.

There is always Hope.

Hope is at the beginning. Hope is not a last resort. The confirmation of "always" means we begin with Hope. Hope does not just show up at the last moment. Hope is always there.

Before the beginning, there was God. It is not that God begins with the beginning of the Universe. There was always God.

With the presence of God, there are always the gifts of grace, peace, and hope. These three. The fuller way to share this reality is this. Before the beginning, there was the God of grace, the Christ of peace, and the Spirit of hope.

The Universe comes into being, blessed, from the very beginning, with grace, peace, and hope, because these three were there before the beginning. The universe stirs and lives forward the grace of God, the peace of Christ, and the hope of the Spirit. The universe has a deep longing and vast yearning to live toward the grace, peace, and hope of God.

You can count on, you can depend on the grace and compassion of God, the peace and contentment of Christ, and the hope and encouragement of the Holy Spirit.

The Universe is not a neutral entity. The Universe favors, leans toward, moves forward, and encourages grace, peace, and hope.

I have been known to say that everything done in human kind is done on hope.

More so, everything done in the Universe is done on Hope. The three life forces, the three dynamics, the three "full of life powers" that stir the Universe are grace, peace, and hope.

We are the people of grace.

We are the people of peace.

We are the people of hope.

Christmas

One sign of the "always" of the grace, peace, and hope of the universe is Christmas. God blesses us with Christmas. Live Christmas. You will live in hope.

Where.

Where Christmas happens is significant. Jesus is born in a manger, not a mansion. This signifies the birth is among the grassroots people of open fields, villages, towns, and cities of the world.

Jesus is born in a cattle stall, not a castle. This confirms that Christ is for the common people, not only the royalty and wealthy. God makes every effort to confirm the every day ordinary life of Jesus. There is no effort to align Christ only with royalty and wealthy.

Jesus is born in a cradle, not a cathedral. This is a simple birth. In a simple place.

There are no frills and fancies. There are no embellishments and flourishes. The birth takes place in a simple stable.

The birth might have taken place in a mansion, a castle, or a cathedral. It is not accidental that it does not. From the very beginning, God wants Christ to share grace that is grass roots, equally available for every person. There is no top down, hierarchical, vertical understanding of grace. Where Jesus is born is significant.

Who Comes.

Who comes to the manger is most important. Who is not there is almost nearly as important. A word, first, on who is not there. There are no kings and emperors. There are no generals. There are no wealthy merchants. The upper strata of society is missing.

It is a simple birth.

The shepherds come. This grouping is among the lowest, poorest groups in the country. They are watching their flocks in the midst of the night. They find their way to the manger. A child is born. They are amazed.

The wise men come. They bring gifts of gold, frankincense, and myrrh. I think of these three gifts as the symbols of grace, peace, and hope. These gifts are now coming into the world in yet more significant and promising ways.

We note that the wise men leave yet another way to avoid any further contact with Herod the Great. This babe is for shepherds and wise men, not kings and emperors.

What Happens.

Grace, Peace, and Hope happen. In the years come and gone, since the birth of Jesus, countless events of grace, rich times of peace, and gracious acts of hope have happened all across the planet. The Birth of the Babe stirs the universe in amazing ways. The power of Christmas is the power of hope.

We are drawn to the manger in much the same ways the shepherds and wise men were drawn. We sense that grace comes down at Christmas, peace stirs across the land, and hope leads us to a new future.

Christmas confirms "the always' of grace, peace, and hope.

Easter

One sign of the "always" of the grace, peace, and hope of the universe is Easter. God blesses us with Easter. Live Easter. You will live in hope.

We are the People of Easter. We are the People of the Open Tomb, the Risen Lord, and New Life and Hope in Christ. We are the People of Everlasting Life.

As strong, healthy persons, we live on hope, live on new life, live on resurrection. We look to the present and the future, not the past. We look to the mission we are sharing now. We experience the spirit of compassion and sense of community in our lives. We focus on the people-centered, person-centered lives of our families and of our communities.

We are discovering new life in the grace of God. We share a spirit of promise. We live as a resurrection people, a people of hope. We live a theology of resurrection, not a theology of retrenchment.

The alarmists do not help us. Their cries of wolf are finally unheeded. Their efforts to frighten and scare are so strident and persistent that we finally quit listening. They are like an obnoxious noise in the background that we simply tune out.

The doomsayers do not advance us. They weigh us down with data and data and data. It is amazing that the early Christian movement flourished without the benefit of computers.

Now, I am for data. I do much research. It is helpful. However, data have their proper and rightful place. Data and demographics are the hirelings to the movement, not its master. We are not here to follow the trends. We are here to change the trends, to advance the trends.

In our time, the old so-called friends of retrenchment and retreat do not help. People are not drawn to groups that include these old friends. They experience enough of retrenchment and retreat in their day-to-day lives. They do not need the mixed blessing of yet another such group that does the same. Sadly, those old friends lead people to a theology of despair.

People are drawn to a grouping that has a theology of incarnation. We discover the grace of God in the manger of Bethlehem. We have a theology of crucifixion. We discover the compassion of Christ, lived out on the cross. But the Christian movement did not end on Golgotha.

We do not hide in an upper room. We do not retreat. We do not bury ourselves in a closed tomb. We do not retrench. We find ourselves in the garden. We discover the open tomb, the Risen Lord, and new life in Christ. Our lives are new and fresh, rich and full.

Regrettably, some people are still at the cross. Worse yet, they may be hiding in an upper room, fearful of a knock on the door, afraid to leave the supposed safety of that dim, dark room. They have not yet found their way, on the first day of the week, to the open tomb and the Risen Lord.

The Gospels are written backward from the experience of the resurrection, from the events of new life and hope. Everything the disciples see, they see finally in the light of the Risen Lord and new life in Christ. In a very real way, we are wise to read the passages about the resurrection, and *then* read the passages about the birth of Jesus.

We are in a resurrection time. The first millennium was the millennium of the incarnation. The second millennium was the millennium of the cross. The third millennium is the millennium of the resurrection.

We are a people of promise, a resurrection people. We have a spirit of wonder and joy, new life and hope. We are the Christmas people. We are the Easter people.

We live in the confidence that God goes before us, as a cloud by day and a fire by night. God is leading us to the future God is promising and preparing for us. God prepares the present and the future.

God is the source of our promise. The source of our promise is not in knowing the lessons of history, nor in projecting the newness of the future. Our promise is not in the pedestals and prerogatives of this world. It is not in the perks and prestige of this world. Our promise is the gift of God. We live with humility and gratitude. We are amazed at God's blessings in our lives. We are amazed at Easter.

Easter confirms "the always' of grace, peace, and hope.

With the grace of God, we discover who we are. We claim our sense of individuality – of identity, integrity, and autonomy.

We find a spirit of community – of roots, place, and belonging – with whom we share life with in God's family.

We develop an understanding of meaning for life – of the value, purpose, and significance of this life.

We look to the present and the future – we live, knowing whose we are – and therefore we live with a strong spirit of hope. We internalize a set of values and standards for our lives. We live whole, healthy lives in grace, peace, and hope.

We are God's people, fashioned by the steadfast love of God. We are God's people, led by the strong hope of God. We live in the grace of God. Love lasts. Hope endures. We live with the assurance of the promise of God. We are the people of promise! We are the people of always.... grace, peace, and hope.

A possibility in coming to understand the gift of hope with which God blesses you is to understand "the Always" of God's gift of hope.

God's gift of hope is not a now and then gift. It is not an off and on gift. It is not sometimes strong and sometimes weak. It is not fragile and feeble, then boisterous and loud. God's gift of hope is strong and solid, stirring and inspiring. Hope stirs the universe. Hope stirs your life.

A BLESSING FOR YOUR LIFE

May the grace of God bless you,
May the joy of grace strengthen you.
May the generosity of God give you grace.
May the community of grace love you.

May the peace of Christ surround you.
May the simplicity of Christ give you peace.
May the health of peace heal you.
May the encouragement of Christ lift you.

May the hope of the Spirit be before you.
May the wisdom of the Spirit guide you.
May the creativity of hope stir you.
May the leading of the Spirit grow you.

May you live in grace, peace, and hope.

Amen.

May God's gift of hope confirm "the Always" of God's gifts in your life.

Encouraging

GOD BLESSES US WITH AN ENCOURAGING SPIRIT.

God blesses us with an encouraging spirit. God is an encouraging God. God encourages us in the present and God looks forward to leading us, with an encouraging spirit, to the life to come. These encouraging possibilities come from the heart of God. These encouraging possibilities include:

Constancy

Grace

Peace

Hope

A Little Girl

Think.... Heart

Seasons

A New Habit

Be at Peace

Head to the Behavior You Want

Sacred

Beginning

Constancy

The Greek Philosopher Heraclites once said, somewhat woefully and somewhat wondrously, "Everything changes."

Another Greek Philosopher, Parmenides, responded, "The constancy is change."

I first learned of this philosophical conversation in my studies with Dr. Joseph Politella of Kent State University. I was privileged to take every course he taught at the university. He is a remarkable influence in my life. He is among the legendary professors of the university. He introduced me to the wondrous world of philosophy.

In the years come and gone, I have reflected on this interchange of these two philosophers. They share helpful wisdom, and I have come to this conclusion,

Heraclites	"Everything changes."
Parmenides	"The constancy is change."
Callahan	"The constancy is grace…peace…hope."

Yes, everything changes. Yes, the constancy is change itself. Yes, the constancy is grace, peace, hope. Before even the universe was born, there was God. With God, there was grace, peace, hope. The constancy is the grace of God, the peace of Christ, and the hope of the Holy Spirit.

Grace

The gift of grace is the gift of compassion, of forgiving, of mercy, of kindness, of love. We are blessed with the grace and compassion of God. Forgiveness and mercy come to us. We receive the forgiving mercy of God. We discover how to forgive persons who have harmed us. We find our way to forgiving ourselves. We live life with the richness of kindness and the depth of love.

The gift of grace overcomes sin, guilt, grudge, bitterness, and resentment. The depth of sin, our sin, overwhelms us. We are grevious for the sin we have done. Our guilt is more than we can bear. We have grudges for the people who have sinned against us. We are bitter. We are resentful.

Grace is life. Life is grace.

Grace thrives, is stirring, vigorous, and abundant. Grace persists, is steadfast, perseveres, refuses to go away. Grace carries on. Grace triumphs.

Life thrives, is stirring, vigorous, and abundant. Life persists, is steadfast, perseveres, refuses to go away, carries on. Life triumphs.

The grace of God comes to us. We are new persons.

Peace

The gift of peace is the gift of calm, of contentment, of community, of serenity, of being relaxed. With the gift of peace, we are calm and contented. We discover roots, place, and belonging. We find family and friends. We are at home. We are at peace.

When we find peace, we find home. When we find home, we find peace.

We are grateful for the amazing gift of peace.

The gift of peace overcomes tense, tight, nervous, and anxious. We are too tense and tight. We have become too nervous and anxious. We allow ourselves to become too worried.

Fear, anxiety, anger, and rage visit us too frequently. Whenever we allow fear to become our companion, anxiety is not far behind. Fear and anxiety breed anger. Fear, anxiety, and anger breed rage. The art is to accept the gift of peace, and to be at peace.

Allow yourself to be at peace.

Peace is a heart thing more than a mind thing. Be at peace in your heart, and then you will be at peace in your mind. Peace has to do with home and forgiveness. Peace is not a thinking quality. Peace is a heart quality.

Hope

The gift of hope is the gift of assurance, of confidence, of an encouraging spirit, of a growing forward in life. The gift of hope overcomes despair, depression, despondency, and defeatism.

Hope is a heart thing more than a mind thing. Live hope in your heart then you will live hope in your mind. Hope has to do with confidence and assurance, an encouraging spirit. Hope is not a thinking quality. Hope is a heart quality.

Some people think something is just around the corner. Some think hope is just around the corner. Some think hope is the corner. In fact, hope is before the corner. Hope is the gift with which we begin.

Hope leads to fishing. Hope leads to casting your nets on right side of boat

A reader in Massachusetts sent the following in to Dear Abby in 2014:

> Take time to work. It is the price of success.
> Take time to think. It is the source of power
> Take time to play. It is the secret of perpetual youth.
> Take time to read. It is the fountain of wisdom.
> Take time to be friendly. It is the road to happiness.
> Take time to love and be loved. It is the privilege of the gods.
> Take time to share. Life is too short to be selfish.
> Take time to laugh. Laughter is the music of the soul.

I would add,
Take time to hope. It is the breath of life.

A Little Girl

A little girl was diligently pounding away on her grandfather's word processor.

She had been hard at it for some time. She told her grandfather she was writing a story.

"What's it about?" he gently asked.

"I don't know," she quietly replied. "I can't read."

She was writing her story. It did not bother her or distress her that she could not read. She was having fun writing her story.

You are welcome to "write your story." You are welcome to give up the word, "no." You are welcome to grow forward your future.

The word "no" denies hope. Hope is more than nope. We spend too much time saying "no." God says "yes" to life. God says "yes" to hope. God encourages us to live with hope.

Sometimes, we are too down on ourselves. We look down on our selves. We think more poorly of ourselves than we have a right to. We suffer from low self esteem. We spend too much time saying "no," "however," "but," "nevertheless," "except," and many other "down-putting" words and thoughts.

Write your story.

Think.... Heart

Think with your heart....Think with your grace.... Think with your peace....Think with your hope.... Feel free to not think with your stress. In 1 Peter 5:7, we discover these words,

"Cast all your anxiety on God because he cares for you."

Hope overcomes anxiety and stress.

Sometimes, we allow stress to preoccupy our lives. We can become better at stress. We can become better at thinking about stress. We can claim the value of a certain amount of stress in our lives. A modest amount of stress helps us to feel free to think about grace, peace, and hope. You can confirm with your self that today is the first day of grace, peace, and hope for the 365 days to come! Think and live, today, in grace, peace, and hope.

Seasons

We can think of **three seasons in our year. We can decide to live:**

the season of grace, September through Christmas
the coming of the Christ Child is the coming of grace

the season of peace, January through Easter
the coming of the Risen Christ is the coming of peace
the resurrection confirms Christ's gift of peace

the season of hope, Easter through August
the coming of Galilee is the coming of hope
Christ goes before us into our Galilee

Life can be these three seasons of the year. We can celebrate that we are the people of grace, peace, and hope.

Living these three seasons helps us to focus on the gifts of grace, peace, and hope, and these three seasons helps us to focus away from a preoccupation with stress, fear, and anxiety. It is not possible, easily, to simply focus away from stress. It helps to put something positive in its place.

A New Habit

It is the old adage of replacing a poor habit with a constructive habit. We replace a preoccupation with stress with a focus on the gifts of grace, peace, and hope with which God blesses us. We do not spend our time saying, "I have got to do something about stress." We focus on practicing the gifts of grace, peace, and hope.

In 2 Corinthians 9:11, we discover these words,

"God will always make you rich enough to be generous at all times,
so that many will thank God for your gifts which they receive from us.

Encouraging

God will make you generous in grace, peace, and hope, and God will make you poor in stress, anxiety, and fear. You will be rich in hope and poor in stress. You will live with confidence and assurance.

Charles Schulz has a wonderful cartoon of Snoopy sitting at his typewriter:

> First panel — Things I've learned after it was too late
> Second panel — A whole stack of memories will never equal one little hope.
> Third panel — Snoopy, looking at what he has typed
> Fourth panel — Snoopy, smiling, I kind of like that.

One little hope helps us to live whole, healthy lives.

Be at Peace

I wrote this saying some time ago,

> When you are worried, gather your mentors.
> When you are anxious, gather your memories.
> When you are stressed, gather your strengths.
> When you are fearful, gather your hope.

Bill Keane of Family Circus has a cartoon. One child says to another child, as both are looking at a flock of birds in the sky,

> What do birds do if they are afraid of flying?
> I add:
> What do fish do, if they are afraid of swimming, of water?
> I add:
> What do humans do, if they are afraid of living, of life?

Be at peace. Birds are at peace about flying. Fish are a peace about swimming. You are welcome to be at peace about living.

Think of it this way. Some persons, hopefully, only a few, spend half of their lives worrying about their living and dying. The irony is that they could have "not been alive" to worry about their dying.

Be at peace. Be grateful you are alive. Be at peace.

Head to the Behavior You Want

Television and radio announcers frequently say, at the time for a commercial:

"Don't go away."

I have always been puzzled by that plea. There are three negatives in that plea:

do not   go   away

The plea teaches people what not to do. The hook is, people go away.

I have often thought that a more constructive invitation would be:

"Stay with us."

There are three positives in this invitation:

stay   with   us

State the behaviour you want in your self, not the behaviour you do not want.

In golfing, I use to say, as the last thought, as I was lining up to hit the ball,

"don't hit it too hard."

The last word in my mind was the word, "hard." Yes, I would hit the ball too hard.

We would now be hunting, searching, here and there, for the lost ball. I learned to say, "Hit the ball easy." Yes, I would have a solid hit.

I find saying, "Be at Peace" more helpful than saying, "Now, don't get angry."

Some people speak fluent sarcasm. I heard this phrase some where.

I add, some people speak fluent depression. Some people speak fluent despair. Some people speak fluent perfectionism.

Some people, in language and behavior, do more than one of the above. They live a dysfunctional duplication that does damage and harm to themselves and to those around them.

I am grateful that many people speak fluent joy and hope. Many people speak fluent grace and peace. Many people speak fluent encouragement and happiness.

What language do you speak?

I am grateful that many people behave with fluent joy and hope. Many people behave with fluent grace and peace. Many people behave with fluent encouragement and happiness.

What behavior, what life do you live?

Head to the language, head to the behavior you want, not the behavior you do not want. You will be an encouraging person in your life.... encouraging with yourself.... encouraging with those around you.

Sacred

Hope is sacred. Hope is a grassroots sacrament. Note well. Grace comes as a babe in a manger, not as a king, a pharaoh, or an emperor. Peace comes as the gift from Jesus, not as a treaty and consortium and declaration. Hope comes as sacred in an empty cross, an open tomb, and new life in grace, peace, and hope.

Hope has a sacramental quality in our lives.

Yes, we experience trials and tribulations in this life. There is:

Fear, Anxiety, Anger, Rage

Misery

Tragedy

Loneliness

Troublement

Defeat, Despair, Disappointment, Depression

Greed, Avarice

Bitterness, Resentment

Stress

Sin, Guilt

Amidst all of these difficulties that beset us, we are blessed with God's wondrous, overflowing, extraordinary, amazing gift of hope.

Winston Churchill once said, "We shape our buildings, thereafter, they shape us."

I say the point this way, "We shape our hopes, thereafter, our hopes shape us." Kennon Callahan

We live on hopes. Our hopes shape how we live.

God blesses us with the sacred, sacramental gift of hope.

Beginning

This is the beginning of your life beyond this book. My hope is that you will live a rich, fill life of grace, peace, and hope.

Hope is not the light at the end of the tunnel. Hope is before the tunnel. Grace, peace, and hope are before the beginnings of the universe.

Christmas is God's way of teaching you your future.

Easter is God's way of teaching you your future.

Encouraging

The stone is rolled away, not so Jesus could get out, but so we could look in. He had already gone, inviting us to the Galilee of our tomorrows.

We have hope in ourselves because we are blessed with the grace of God, the peace of Christ, and the hope of the Holy Spirit. God blesses us with grace, peace, and hope so we will have personal hope in ourselves.

God invites you to live a hope filled life, an encouraging life. Not necessarily ever brimming, brimming over with hope. Hope is sometimes shy, bashful, and modest.

Hope and humility are good friends. Hope does not boast, is not loud, does not brag, does not show off. Hope is resilient, solid, tough.

A possibility for growing the gift of hope with which God blesses you is to live an encouraging life. Persons who live a life of encouragement live a life of hope. Some persons lack encouragement; they lack hope.

God blesses us with an encouraging spirit. God is an encouraging God. God encourages us in the present. God leads us forward, with an encouraging spirit, in the life to come.

Encouragement is a wondrous gift of God that stirs our best selves to move forward.

God gives us the gift of encouragement so we can live with hope.

>   Grace is stronger than law.
>   Compassion is stronger than selfishness.
>   Peace is stronger than fear.
>   Community is stronger than loneliness, isolation.
>
>   Hope is stronger than despair.
>   Challenge is stronger than defeat.
>   Reasonability is stronger than confusion.
>   Commitment is stronger than betrayal.

Do not conform to the pattern of this world but be ye transformed
by the renewing of your mind.
>   Romans 12:2 Bible

Do not conform to the pattern of this world but be ye transformed
by the renewing of your heart, and
by the renewing of your hope.
>   Callahan

God's Generous Gift

GOD BLESSES US WITH MANY POSSIBILITIES FOR HOPE

Generous Possibilities

God's generous gift of hope is so generous that God blesses us with all of these possibilities with which we can live in hope. God is eager for us to live lives of hope. The art is to select a possibility that will help you to live your life in hope.

>God blesses us with Persons of Hope.
>God encourages us to discover Persons of Hope.
>God invites you to be a Person of Hope.

>God blesses you with strengths.
>God blesses you with motivations.
>God blesses you with generosity.
>God blesses you with passion.

>God blesses you with your memories.
>God blesses you with your mentors.
>God blesses you with some changes.
>God blesses us with outcomes.

> God blesses you with Hope beyond War
> God blesses you with the wonders, power, and joy of Hope.
> God blesses you with Nets
>
> Gossip, Apathy, Generations
> Always
> Encouraging
> God's Generous Gift

I have shared these possibilities so you can discover one or two possibilities that match best with you. Do not try to do all of them. That effort would be a sign of a compulsive addictive perfectionism, and that would not lead to a life of hope.

Live one or two possibilities. Live in hope.

Hope is Universal

God plants the longing for hope in every human heart. God plants the yearning for hope in every culture and in every civilization. All human beings and all cultures and all ages have a deep longing for hope.

All peoples have understandings of hope. Given the age and given the culture, there is a longing and yearning for the gift of hope. Across the ages of humanity, there have been many searchings to discover hope.

Recently, in my research for this book, I reread the legend of hope found in Greek culture.... the legend of Pandora and her Box. This is among the classic legends of hope.

Pandora was to keep the Box, actually it was a Jar, as a trust. It was not a gift. It was a trust to be kept safe. Epimetheus, her husband, reminded Pandora that she was to keep the Jar as a sacred trust.

Regrettably, one day, Pandora's husband left her side for a short time.

As the legend has it, Pandora was gifted with the gift of curiosity as well as the other gifts given her by the gods. For her, the Jar was a gift, not something to be kept in trust. Her curiosity began to get the best of her.

Maybe, she could take a quick peak.... just a quick peak.

Being sure that no one was watching, she opened the Jar.... just a crack.

.... Just a crack.

.... Ghostly forms gushed forth from the crack.

Pandora had unleashed all the evils now present and known to human kind. No longer could human kind laze about all day. Now, he would have to work and would succumb to all of the evils and perils and illnesses of human kind.

For a long time, I had thought this was the end of the legend. Pandora had unleashed all the perils and evils in humanity.

This is not the end of the parable. Note well.

The legend continues.

At the very bottom of the Jar was the last thing to come out. It was something that was not evil. We call the good thing that Pandora unleashed by the name of hope.

Amidst all of the evils that had escaped, the key to the legend is that ***hope is now present in humankind.*** Pandora had turned hope loose in the world.

Yes, many civilizations have a longing and understanding of hope. Hope is universal. Hope is among the deep longings and yearnings of all humanity.

We live on hope. We live in hope.

In an earlier time, in the time of Rome, hope was built on the conviction, "Rome is eternal." For days upon days, years, decades, and centuries, the phrase of hope was "Rome is eternal." Roads were built. Armies marched. Merchants sailed. Cities were erected.

The confidence, the hope, was "Rome is eternal."

All civilizations, all cultures, all peoples cast about for some symbol of hope. For the people of that ancient time, the symbol of hope was Rome.

Rome fell.

Our hope had been in Rome. What now is our hope?

All ages seek hope. Sometimes, we seek a new Rome, only to see it fall.

Hope is not finally in the "stuff, the glories, the power, the majesties, the pomp and ceremonies we fabricate and conjure up.

Grace, peace, and hope are eternal.

> The stirring, moving grace of God is eternal.
> The calming, comforting peace of Christ is eternal.
> The leading, encouraging hope of the Holy Spirit is eternal.

God is before the beginning. Grace, peace, and hope are before the beginning. Technically, grace, peace, and hope are before eternal. For Pandora, hope comes at the end, at the bottom of the Jar, in a smaller spirit. At least, for Pandora hope comes.

For us, hope comes before the beginning. Hope comes in generous, full, rich, amazing strength. Hope comes as God's overwhelming, larger than the universe gift to you. God gives you the amazing, generous gift of hope.

Yes, you and I might be tempted to lessen and diminish the fullness of God's gift.

Even as we might do so, God continues to give us the gift of hope, with amazing generosity.

Hope and Heaven

Hope and Heaven are good friends.

God's generous gift is Hope. Hope and Heaven go together.

God longs for you to receive the gift of hope in this life. God yearns for you to have the gift of hope in the life to come. God is more interested in Hope and Heaven than in Hell.

Now, Heaven is hell for the people who are in Heaven and do not understand what Heaven is about. Heaven is about grace, peace, and hope. Heaven is a people and a place of grace and compassion, peace and contentment, hope and encouragement.

Heaven is not about glory and status, power and prestige, and majesty and caste systems. Heaven is grassroots. When one brings their own fear, despair, bitterness, resentment, anger, and depression with them to Heaven, they will be in a Hell of their own making, in Heaven. They will not know they are in Heaven.

People create the Hells of their own making. In our present life and in our life to come, we create our own Hell by wallowing in our own self-created fear, anxiety, anger, rage, bitterness, resentment, despair, depression, dejection, and despondency.

The irony is that we are in Heaven and we bring our own little Hell along with us. Surrounded by the beauty of Heaven, we fabricate our own little Hell. We are our own worst enemy. We seek to quell our deep-seated fear with efforts of glory, power, and majesty. We falsely imagine we can quiet our fear with symbols of glory, power, and majesty.

In the midst of our feeble efforts, God longs to.... seeks to.... yearns to give us.... generously and fully.... the generous gifts of grace, peace, and hope.

"Therefore, since we have been justified by faith, we have peace with God through our Lord Jesus Christ. Through him we have also obtained access by faith into this grace in which we stand, and we rejoice in hope of the glory of God."

Romans 5:1-2

Living in Hope

Hope is as natural as the universe. Hope is as natural as breathing. Hope is as natural as the sunrise. Hope is generously present as God's gift to you. God longs for and yearns for you to live in hope.

God's gift of hope is so powerful, so persuasive, so stirring that it only takes selecting one or two of the possibilities shared in ***Living in Hope*** and the gift of hope comes rushing in, pouring in, and flowing fully into your life. You will live with much joy and grace, peace and hope.

With all of these possibilities, all of these gifts of hope, it is a puzzle that some people do not live in hope. It is a puzzle that some people choose to live in despair.

It takes much more energy to live in despair. To live in despair is to live "against the grain" of life God gives us. To live in despair is to live "against the life force of the universe."

It takes enormous energy to live over against all of these possibilities, and decide to live in despair, depression, dejection, and despondency.

People are not born in despair. People learn despair. People work hard to live in despair. People become tired, fatigued, and worn out living in despair.

God's Generous Gift

My thought is that some persons convince themselves, wrongly, again I say wrongly, that they are not worthy of the gift of hope.

They look down on themselves. They think more poorly of themselves than they have a right to. They suffer from low self esteem. They suffer from fear. Thus, they fail to accept the blessing of God's gift of hope.

Living in hope is "living with the grain."

The universe lives in hope.

Living in hope is "living with the universe."

Look at the sky and see the hope of God. Look at the stars and see the hope of God. Look at the movement of life around you and see the hope of God.

Look at the Persons of Hope with whom God blesses you and see the hope of God. Look at the life of Christ and see the hope of God. Look at when you act like a Person of Hope and see the hope of God.

> God blesses you with the gift of hope.
> God gives you all of these possibilities so you can choose one or two, and, thereby, live in hope.
> This day, live in hope.

God's generous gift is for you to live a life in hope.
God encourages you to choose
any of these possibilities so you will live in hope.
God blesses you with hope.
Accept God's gift of hope.
Live in hope.
May grace, peace, and hope bless you always.
Amen.

Hope is beyond the end of forever....

Hope is God's Gift with us.
Hope is not some sentiment we manufacture.
Hope is not some cause we somehow stir up within us.
Hope comes from God as God's generous gift.

Hope is happy, not sad.
Hope is glad, not mad.
Hope is sensible.
Hope is immeasurable.
Hope goes on.
Hope moves forward.

Hope sees beyond.
Hope is before the beginning.
Hope is the beginning.
Hope is beyond the beyond.
Hope never ends.
Hope endures.
Hope endures beyond endures.
Hope lasts....beyond the end of forever....

When your job becomes your life, you no longer have a life.
Life is more than a job. Hope is more than a job.

God's Generous Gift

Hope stirs action. Hope stirs dreams.
Hope and dreams stir action.

Hope is not something we think.
Hope is something we love.

We are blessed with grace.
We are at peace.
We live in hope.

Grace endures.
Peace quiets.
Hope lives beyond the end of forever.

Kennon L. Callahan

About the Author

DR. KENNON L. CALLAHAN, PH. D.

Kennon L. Callahan - author, researcher, professor, theologian, and pastor - is a number one bestselling author and among today's most sought-after speakers and consultants.

Dr. Callahan's newest and twenty first book is **Living in Hope**.

He has worked with thousands of groupings around the world and has helped tens of thousands of persons and leaders. His helpful seminars are filled with encouragement, compassion, wisdom, and practical possibilities.

Dr. Callahan's research travels have led him to all of the states in the United States, all of the provinces in Canada, the Arctic, Norway, Holland, England, Denmark, Sweden, Finland, Estonia, Germany, Russia, Turkey, Greece, Italy, Spain, France, Egypt, Lebanon, Palestine, Jordan, Israel, Mexico, the British Virgin Islands, the Bahamas, Chile, Brazil, and the Antarctica. His current research interests are in both cultural archaeology and in human behavior.

Author of many books, he is best known for his groundbreaking **Twelve Keys to an Effective Church**, which has formed the basis for the widely acclaimed Mission Growth Movement, which is helping many persons across the planet.

In the Order of DeMolay, he was elected Master Councilor of the second largest DeMolay Chapter in North America. He earned the

Degree of Representative DeMolay. He was awarded the Degree of Chevalier. Later, he was elected to the Degree of Legion of Honor.

Dr. Callahan has earned the Bachelor of Arts degree, the Master of Divinity degree, the Master of Sacred Theology degree, and the Doctor of Philosophy degree.

He has studied Latin, Greek, Hebrew, French, German, and Australian.

In 1959, he was elected and ordained to the Ministry Order of Deacon in the United Methodist Church. In 1962, he was elected and ordained to the Ministry Order of Elder in the United Methodist Church.

He has served as a pastor of rural and city congregations in Ohio, Texas, and Georgia. He taught for many years at Emory University.

Dr. Callahan is the founder of the Continuing Education Center for Candler School of Theology, the founder of the North Georgia Teaching Parish, and the founder of the National Certification Program in Church Finance and Administration.

He is the founder of Church Records Management, one of the earliest computer based companies serving congregations. He was given the Distinguished Alumni Award of Cuyahoga Falls High School. He was elected to the Hall of Fame by the National Association of Church Business Administrators. He is the founder of the National Institute for Church Planning, and serves as Consultant with many congregations and denominations.

His recent books, **Living in Grace** and **Living in Peace**, are helping many persons across the planet. Three recent books include the new edition of **Twelve Keys to an Effective Church,** the new edition of the **Twelve Keys Leaders' Guide,** and the new **Twelve Keys Bible Study.** Altogether, he is the author of twenty one books.

While in high school, Ken enlisted in the United State Navy, in the Naval Reserve. He completed Boot Camp at the Great Lakes

About the Author

Naval Training Center near Chicago, Illinois. He spent time serving aboard the U.S.S. Stephen Potter in the Atlantic Ocean. He taught the advanced course of Seaman Apprenticeship II.

Ken and Julie, his wife, met in high school in January of 1954. Julie invited Ken to a square dance at her church. They began dating, went steady, became engaged, and married. They celebrated the sixty first anniversary of their first date on January 31, 2015. They celebrated the fifty ninth anniversary of their wedding on August 11, 2015.

He put his way through the university by working, first, for Harry Miller Construction Company, then, for Lomelo Contracting Company. He started as a ditch digger, worked up to running a ninety pound jack hammer; then, finally became a form setter for highways, streets, cutters, driveways, and sidewalks.

He also worked for the Registrars Office at the university. Ken and Julie served as Sextons for the Wesley Foundation House during his junior year. He served the Mountville and Thompson congregations during this time.

In his senior year, they were the first pastoral couple to live in Brady Lake and to serve the Brady Lake church. While there, they and the congregation built a parsonage so the church could have a continuous ministry presence across the years.

Ken and Julie are thankful for the many friends they share across the planet. They have two excellent sons, Ken, Jr., and Michael, a wonderful daughter-in-law, Shay, married to Ken, Jr., and three grandsons: Blake, Mason, and Brice. They share good fun and good times with the outdoors, hiking, camping, reading, researching, traveling, quilting, sailing, and visiting with their friends. They enjoy being with one another.

Ken is a Senior in 1954
Julie is a Sophomore in 1954

Ken and Julie Callahan are visiting friends in the Shenandoah Valley of Virginia, enjoying the Blue Ridge Mountains with the Skyline Drive meandering along the ridges.

The picture is taken at the Rivers Bend Ranch of Elaine and Mac McConnell, outside of Stanley, Virginia. Richard Worden, their long time, good friend, is taking the picture.

Richard has written of Ken and Julie, "The history and beauty of the Valley grace their lives even as they have graced the lives of friends, colleagues and congregations for decades."

Bibliography of the Books by the Author

DR. KENNON L. CALLAHAN, PH.D.

Living in Hope ISBN-10:1516998847

God blesses you with the gift of hope. God blesses you with many possibilities with which you can live a life of hope. Select a possibility most helpful to you. Enjoy living a life in hope.

Living in Peace ISBN 978-1491088753

An encouraging, helpful book that shares possibilities for living in peace. Discover ten helpful events. Discover wonderful persons in Eunice, Mrs. Perkins, Gene, Charles, Ken, Opal, Grandma Ida and Kate, Mom, Mimi, Aunt Bea, St. John's, Dorothy, Grand Children, Orville, and Ken and Julie. Discover peace. Live in grace and peace.

Living in Grace ISBN 978-1481200882

A joyful, encouraging book that shares possibilities for living in grace. Discover twelve decisive events. Discover remarkable persons of grace. Strengthen your living in grace. You will find this book helpful in your own life—living in grace.

Twelve Keys to an Effective Church: Strong, Healthy Congregations Living in the Grace of God, Second Edition   ISBN 978-0-470-55929-1

For the first time in print, the five basic qualities for strong, healthy congregations. New possibilities for an effective, successful congregation. New suggestions for expanding your current strengths and adding new strengths. New wisdom and insights on mission, sacrament, and grace. The book helps you to be a mission growth congregation.

The Twelve Keys Leaders' Guide: An Approach for Grassroots, Key Leaders, and Pastors Together   ISBN 978-0-470-55928-4

Lead your congregation in developing a strong, healthy future. Excellent ideas and good suggestions on how to lead a helpful *Twelve Keys* planning retreat. Resources for encouraging action, implementation, and momentum. Insights on the dynamics of memory, change, conflict, and hope in congregations. An excellent companion for the new *Twelve Keys* book.

The Twelve Keys Bible Study   ISBN 978-0-470-55916-1

Biblical resources for the *Twelve Keys*. Scriptures for each of the *Twelve Keys* and reflections on these scriptures. Suggestions and questions for study and conversation. Helpful for Advent and Lenten Bible studies, and for preaching and worship services. An excellent companion Bible study for the new *Twelve Keys* book.

The Future That Has Come   ISBN 0 7879 49817

The seven major paradigm shifts of recent years. New possibilities for reaching and growing the grassroots. Motivating and leading your congregation.

Small, Strong Congregations   ISBN 0 7879 49809

The distinctive dynamics of small, strong congregations. Ministers, leaders, and members of small congregations develop a strong, healthy future together.

A New Beginning for Pastors and Congregations   ISBN 0 7879 42898

What to do in the first three months of a new pastorate; how to make a new start in a present pastorate.

Preaching Grace   ISBN 0 7879 42952

Develop an approach to preaching that matches your own distinctive gifts. Help your preaching share the spirit of grace with your people,

Twelve Keys for Living   ISBN 0 7879 41409

Claim the strengths for living that God gives you. Develop a whole, healthy life. Solid Lenten or Advent study.

Visiting in an Age of Mission   ISBN 0 7879 38688

Develop shepherding in your congregation. Groupings to shepherd. The variety of ways you can shepherd.

Effective Church Finances   ISBN 0 7879 38696

Develop an effective budget, set solid giving goals, and increase the giving of your congregation.

Dynamic Worship   ISBN 0 7879 38661

Major resources for stirring, inspiring worship services, helpful and hopeful in advancing people's lives.

Giving and Stewardship   ISBN 0 7879 3867X

   Grow generous givers. Motivations out of which people give. Six primary sources of giving. Giving principles in generous congregations. How to encourage your whole giving family.

Effective Church Leadership   ISBN 0 7879 38653

   Foundational life searches. Seven best ways to grow leaders. Develop constructive leadership.

Building for Effective Mission   ISBN 0 7879 38726

   Develop your mission. Evaluate locations. Maximize current facilities. Building new space.

   Create an effective building team. Selecting an architect. Develop an extraordinary first year.

Twelve Keys to an Effective Church   ISBN 0 7879 38718

   Claim your current strengths, expand some, and add new strengths to be a strong, healthy congregation. Encourage your whole congregation to study this book—it helps in their church, family, work, and life.

Twelve Keys: The Planning Workbook   ISBN 0 7879 38734

   Each person contributes directly to creating an effective long-range plan for your future together.

Twelve Keys: The Leaders' Guide   ISBN 0 7879 3870x

   How to lead your congregation in developing an effective plan for your future. How to develop action, implementation, and momentum. Dealing with the dynamics of memory, change, conflict, and hope.

Twelve Keys: The Study Guide　　　　　　　　ISBN 0 7879 39420

An excellent Bible study of the *Twelve Keys*, with helpful resources and solid discussion possibilities.

God bless you with Hope.
Amen.